I'M YOURS

I'M YOURS

Based on a True Story

M W

While the story is true, all names have been changed and various events slightly altered to protect the identity and well-being of individuals involved.

Printed in the United States of America

First Printing, 2015

ISBN 0692546170
ISBN 13: 9780692546178

ACKNOWLEDGEMENTS

I never had any intention of publishing my story, or even telling any-one my story at all. After several years, though, I felt that what I had suffered still haunted me. The beginning of this journey started in an English class in college. We were instructed to write a ten page pa-per about anything of our choosing. It didn't take me long to decide that I wanted to write about my abusive relationship during my fresh-man year of high school. The words poured onto the pages, and after I was through with the assignment, I felt a sense of relief. My English professor was so impressed with my paper that he recommended that I write a book. I started writing slowly, painfully recording the memo-ries I forced myself to relive. I wrote bits and pieces during breaks from school, never really imagining that I would ever finish writing. Writing became a source of therapy for me. I never really saw my story traveling any further until I learned that the boy that used to put his hands around my neck had been abusing his current girlfriend – just like he had abused me. I hated myself for not putting him in jail when I had the chance, and decided that my story could give hope and strength to those in similar situations. I want to thank my friends who believed in me, supported me, and encouraged me through this entire process – without you, this wouldn't have been possible.

PROLOGUE

I laid under clothes and broken shelves in the closet, hiding from him and hoping that he had forgotten where he had left me. I felt like I had been there for days, but I assumed it had just been a few hours. My head was hurting too badly to judge how much time had passed. My heart hurt worse than my head did, though, and my eyes were raw from the tears I had cried until I couldn't cry any more. I watched blood from my nose drip onto the white carpet. Before I met Collin, that would have been something that I would have actually cared about. Stains were the least of my problems, though. I just stared at it, worrying about what was to come when Collin came back. I curled myself into a ball and held my ripped shirt over my back, picturing the rage flaring in his eyes and trying to pinpoint the exact moment that caused what happened that night.

I always believed that everything was my fault. That's what he told me, at least, and his voice was the only thing I listened to. I thought that I deserved to be punished because despite my best effort, I couldn't make him happy. Ways to apologize to him would circle through my mind every time he got mad. I never understood what I did to deserve the things he did to me.

I started to wonder where everyone from my past life was and what they were doing. At the time, I believed that I abandoned all of my friends and family to be with Collin, but now I know that he tore me from them and everything else I loved. He stripped me of my identity so all I knew was him. I wanted him to hold me and take away my pain, but deep down I knew that I needed to escape him. I felt my body go numb as the front door opened. I cringed as I heard footsteps approaching closer. I was scared for my life. I knew that nothing was stopping him from putting those big hands around my neck again. My whole body was sore, but I lifted myself up as the closet door opened. A dark figure stood in the doorway staring at my pitiful, bruised self.

I called out his name, but he didn't say anything. Finally he spoke, and it was Joey, the person who we went to visit that night. "No, he's gone. What happened?" I couldn't form words. I threw my arms around him and started crying all over again. I felt guilty for being so relieved that it wasn't my boyfriend standing in the doorway. I felt even guiltier that I knew what Collin would do to Joey if he found out that he held me like he did. My sense of right and wrong had been altered, though, and I wasn't sure what I was supposed to feel. Joey told me that his sister called him begging him to come home. She was the only one there when the fight started, and her swollen eye was a symbol of her bravery for standing up for me.

I had no intention of the night ending how it did. I hated myself for allowing things to get so bad. I thought about running away as I had before, but I got scared. I knew his punishment for that would be worse than the fight we were having. Nobody wanted me to be with him, but nobody stuck around long enough for me to feel like I could leave him. By the time I was ready to be done with him, I had no one and nothing. He was all I had, and I clung to the only thing that let me. I can't say that I didn't understand why my friends and family had pulled away. I had always blamed girls for not leaving relationships similar to the one I was in. I never had any sympathy for girls that would continuously put themselves in dangerous situations. I called them stupid until I knew how it felt – how difficult it really is to leave. There's so much emotion invested into that one person. It was a constant battle of hope and fear.

It was a new year, also marking the anniversary of me and Collin. I knew that Collin wasn't good for me. I knew that I needed to leave him. He threatened me, though, and I didn't take those threats lightly. He gave me some hope as he promised me he would never hurt me again. He swore that he wasn't cheating on me anymore. I acted like I believed him, but I knew better. There was nothing I could do to stop it. I had become desensitized to the cheating after so long and after so many graphic details of his nights with other girls, but his anger was something that I could never grow to accept. At 15 years old I felt my body grow weaker every time he had an episode. I imagined him slamming my head into the wall just a little too hard or choking me just a little too long. I knew he would kill me someday.

Our relationship hadn't always been so miserable. I hadn't always been so fragile. In fact, when he met me, I was incredibly strong and stable. I was a freshman in high school, a cheerleader with the right grades and motivation to take me far in life. My first semester of high school had been ideal. Collin slithered into my life late December, and after that it didn't take long for everything to come crashing down around me. Going to high school made me a little boy crazy. Collin was the first to take interest in me, and I loved his attention.

With harsh tones and degrading looks, I often got asked why I stayed with him for so long. Although I knew the answer to that, I always told them that I didn't know. I silently thought that they would have stayed too, because it isn't as simple as they believed it to be. I knew why he had such a hold on me for so long, but it was too complicated for any of them to understand. It was hard to believe that our relationship went to such extremes. At times, I closed my eyes to reality, myself. I didn't want to believe that something so pure and perfect turned cold and hateful. Collin opened up a very dark box inside of my soul, and I hated him for it. I also desperately needed him. He unraveled me so that I could only be put back together by him. The butterflies in my stomach eventually turned into bruises around my arms. Being with him was a constant roller-coaster of emotions that turned into something scary. There's a moment when riding on a roller-coaster that the cart is upside down for a split second. That second is filled with fear yet still incredibly exciting. That's the moment that hooks people. That rush of emotions is what makes people get back on. That is what I felt with Collin.

1

PURITY

When I met Collin, everyone saw the bad in him except for me. I had always looked at the world from a scope of beauty. I hated negativity, and I had always felt as if I was someone who could lessen the bad in the world. During my freshman year of high school, that innocent little spark I had was killed.

I was terrified to go to high school. I begged my mom to let me stay home. I was scared of what people would think of me. I thought high school was the most important thing in life. My friends believed that life was over after high school. I basically had to be dragged out of the car on the first day of school. It slowly got better and I got more comfortable with friends that I thought were forever. We roamed the halls with increasing ease and cheered at football and basketball games with confidence. We were closer than ever, and I couldn't be happier. I had a carefree life.

With the first break of our first semester of high school coming up, we had big plans. Our Thanksgiving break consisted of sleep-overs that we didn't actually sleep at, watching scary movies, and talking about boys. We had all been involved in the middle-school relationships that we thought were real before going to high school, but we dreamed of more. The last weekend of our break, we got a glimpse of what we innocently giggled about for weeks. We all went to Abby's house for our last event of the break. After her parents had gone to sleep, two senior boys showed up. I had grown boy-obsessed in the past couple of months. The senior boys were not only incredibly attractive, but they had something about them that our freshman boys lacked. They seemed to have everything all figured out, and I had two right in front of me. It seemed like any other night, just with a little bit of an edge. My life completely changing following that night was the last thing I expected to happen. I never thought that such a simple moment could take away everything familiar to me. I had no idea that I was about to meet the person that would make me feel things I didn't know I could feel. Then he introduced himself.

Something about Collin pulled me in instantly. His eyes captured every part of myself that I was terrified to give to someone else. His overwhelming confidence entranced me, and I was in no hurry to break it. We all sat in a circle and talked for hours. I was sitting in-between Collin and his friend, Jaret, staying awake as long as I could so I wouldn't miss anything. Collin seemed to take a personal interest in me, talking to me more than he was the rest of the group. They left before Abby's parents woke up, and I evaluated the night in my head until falling asleep.

I thought little of my night with the two senior boys until a few days later when I saw Collin in the school hallway. For the next week, I went out of my way to pass him between classes. My best friend, April, caught on, and encouraged me to talk to him. Asking him for his jacket could be seen as both innocent and playful, and it would give me an actual reason to talk to him. There was little intimidation involved, and it also would give me an excuse to see him again – I would have to return the jacket. I followed through with my plan. Trying to look cold in my cheerleading uniform, I got some courage and approached him. April watched as I walked up to him and asked him if he remembered me in my cute, innocent voice.

"Yeah, Mikayla, is it?"

I corrected him. "It's McKenzie, actually, but I was just wondering if you happened to have an extra jacket. It's so cold in this school."

"Yeah I do," he said with a sly smile. He set down his backpack and pulled out a jacket, handing it to me.

He asked me for my number so he could get his jacket back, and I gave it to him. He texted me shortly after and our conversations quickly got personal. He told me that he was going through a breakup, and that I was easy to talk to. By the end of that conversation, I believed that his ex-girlfriend was heartless. His account of the breakup was that she cheated on him for the two years that they were together, and he was completely heartbroken. He made it seem as if he was loyal and forgiving, but finally had to break things off with her – he just couldn't take the heartache anymore. I couldn't believe that someone would do that to him. I hated the picture he painted of her. Her name is Amanda, and she ended up playing a much bigger part in my life than I ever imagined.

I wore Collin's jacket proudly until I had to cheer at a basketball game that night. April and Hallie took notice of my good mood. I was so excited that a senior boy was texting me. I tried not to get my hopes up and took part in complaining about the basketball game with the rest of the girls. I yelled our cheers with a bigger smile and clapped my hands with more enthusiasm than usual. High school had been great for me, and I thought it was only going to get better.

I was doing math homework the next night when Collin texted me about getting his jacket back. He wanted to come pick it up from my house, so I told him my address and that I was doing homework, so he couldn't stay. He offered to tutor me, and with his slight hint of interest, I accepted his offer. I didn't really need the help, but I wanted to see him. It also gave me an excuse to be alone with him for the first time. He arrived shortly after our conversation. I met him at his truck and he surprised me with a Cotton Candy Blizzard from Dairy Queen. I invited him inside, and when he refused my offer, I brought his jacket and my homework out to his truck. He looked over my homework, and tried to explain the math to me. I pretended that he was actually helping me, but everything he was saying was wrong.

I ate my blizzard and promised myself I would fix my math home-work when he left. We sat in his beat up truck in my driveway until he finally had to go home. I loved that he didn't make me nervous. Normally I would have frozen and acted like an idiot around a guy I liked. With Collin, I could talk to him like we had been friends for years. He had this charm that made me feel comfortable with him. He texted me from when he got home until I fell asleep. I woke up the next morning with more confidence than I had since high school started. I couldn't wrap my mind around the fact that it was actually happening – a senior boy was actually showing interest in me.

Collin came over again the next night to "tutor" me with another Blizzard from Dairy Queen. We talked less about math than we did the night before. This became a nightly thing, and every night we would talk less about math and more about ourselves. Every night he played his music a little louder and I found myself laughing with him a little bit more. Our nightly sit-outs in my driveway turned into driving around the town. He looked at me instead of the road, charming me with that perfect smile and those gorgeous blue eyes. He sang loudly to his music while I giggled out loud. I liked his bold, obnoxious personality. It was what I needed to get me to break out of my shy shell. "I'm Yours" by Jason Mraz came on his radio, and I couldn't resist singing with him. I knew after singing that song together that we would be something more. I tossed and turned all that night with butterflies in my stomach. My middle school relationships couldn't even compare to him. He was older and more mature, and that would make it real with him. I couldn't screw it up – it was too perfect.

It was finally Christmas break. I had survived my first semester of high school. With Collin's mom working, we had his house to our-selves. He invited his friend, Jeremy over, and Jeremy brought his girl-friend, Kate. She was in the same grade as me, but we barely knew each other. Collin's arms were locked around me and he whispered sweet things in my ear throughout the night. I couldn't get enough. When I assumed my mom would start worrying soon, I asked to go home. Jeremy drove us and dropped me off at the end of my road. As

I was scooting out of Jeremy's truck, Collin grabbed my arm. I turned around as he put his hand on the back of my head through my hair and kissed me. I saw fireworks and felt something I had never felt before. It was irrevocable. I was in love with him. Nothing else mattered. It was us against the world. I stumbled out of Jeremy's truck and almost fell on my face. Collin reached down to help me up, trying not to laugh. I was mortified, but I laughed at myself anyway. I walked inside and screamed in excitement after making sure the door was closed.

A few days later we joined April and her boyfriend Justin at a party at Justin's house for New Year's. We stayed alone for most of the night. I sat with him in the back of his truck, shivering, as we watched the fireworks. He held me closely while we looked at the sky, and the bursts of light and color made me feel so open to anything and everything with him. I felt vulnerable. It was scary, but I liked it. He told me everything he liked about me, and he asked me if I would be his girlfriend. I didn't have to think about it – I automatically said yes. I wanted nothing more than to be with him. He made me feel like the luckiest girl in the world.

2

ENVY

It was my first Valentine's Day with a boyfriend and I couldn't have been more excited. Collin hadn't brought up plans, so I figured that there would be a surprise planned for me. I curled my hair and put on my makeup with a little extra effort that day. I went to his house after school and walked in without knocking. We had only been official for about a month, and I expected a box of chocolates, a card, something. He kept his eyes glued on the TV as I walked to the couch to join him. I asked if we were doing anything later in a disappointed tone, and he shrugged his shoulders.

He agreed to take me to dinner, and I ignored the fact that he invited Jeremy. I grew excited until we walked in. He brought me to a cheap, small, Italian restaurant that served what looked like frozen dinners. I tried to hide the fact that I was incredibly annoyed, and my frustration grew even stronger as my food came out with meat on it. I hadn't eaten meat in years, and I didn't plan to start eating it again that night. Collin's frustration matched mine when I refused to eat the food he bought. He ignored me for the rest of the night to talk to Jeremy across the table. I stared at my food, untouched, until we left. When we got in the truck I accused him of not caring and he accused me of expecting too much. I crossed my arms and looked out the window, refusing to give in and apologize. We didn't talk for the rest of the night.

With our tension unresolved, I began to grow worried. We were care-free when we first met, and in such a short time it had started to deteriorate. I wasn't ready to let him go. We had so much fun being together in the beginning, and I held onto those memories. Sometimes I forgot how much our age difference affected our relationship. I was hesitant as he slowly dragged me onto an experience level much more suited for his age than mine. I got news that he was going elsewhere when I would tell him no. I knew he was getting bored with me. I spent more and more nights alone as he was doing things with other girls I didn't want to think about. I promised myself that the next time we were together, I would finally say yes. I didn't make that promise out of love or trust, but out of fear of losing him, or maybe out of wanting to be better than the other girls he entertained himself with. I kept my promise, realizing that deep down it wasn't a good idea. Deep down I knew that I could never give him enough to fully satisfy him, but it didn't stop me from trying. He held me tight and slowly kissed me all night. I had never felt closer to anyone before in my life. Girls no longer shared something with Collin that I didn't – I had it all.

Every time we were intimate with each other, the more I enjoyed it and the less careful we got. We had few boundaries – we didn't care who was at his house or who could walk in. One day Jeremy came into Collin's bedroom while he was still getting dressed. He told me that I should claim Collin, laughing and handing me a permanent marker. Collin pulled down his pants and I wrote "McKenzie was here" in a place that I thought no one else would see.

I found out the next day at school that I didn't have to tell my friends for them to find out what I did. The whole school had found out sometime between Sunday afternoon and 3rd period Monday morning. I didn't know how anyone could have possibly found out, and I didn't know what to say to my friends. My friendship with them had been hanging on by a thread, and that thread had been cut the second they heard about my first Collin-related scandal. At lunch I tried to tell Hallie that it was just a joke, and she told me that her group of friends couldn't afford to associate with a whore. With tears in my eyes I texted Collin to meet me in our usual spot by the lockers. I told him that I couldn't understand why people were making such a big deal of our little joke – a lot of girls had done way worse things and didn't get criticized as badly as I was. He told me that they were jealous, and that he would take care of it. He held me tightly and kissed me on the forehead, promising that he would make it better. I liked the thought of people being jealous of us, and I considered it as a real possibility. What I liked even more, though, was the feeling that I could count on Collin to stand up for me. I had completely lost every single friend I had with the exception of April, but even she was a little hesitant to talk to me.

Collin's mom was almost never home, so we had a lot of uninterrupted alone time in his bedroom. His TV was on when we walked into his bedroom. I noticed him paying more attention to the TV than to me. I was already insecure. He was way more experienced than I was, and I felt like I was in constant competition with not only every girl he had been with in the past, but every girl he encountered in the present and future. I felt like I had to be the very best, although I didn't know how to be. Everything made me question my performance. I got reassurance when he cuddled with me after, and I took it hard when he went to parties with his friends without me. I rudely told him that he needed to turn off the TV.

"Why?" Collin asked me, still looking at the TV. I got off of him and started putting on my clothes. "What's your problem McKenzie?" I rolled my eyes and walked out of the room. He followed me, frustrated. "You're seriously just going to stop during the middle of it?" He asked me, raising his voice. I answered with another question, raising my voice to match his. "You're seriously going to watch TV while I'm on top of you?" "It wasn't a big deal for Amanda," he told me. That made me even more insecure. I felt hot, but I kept my cool. He could tell that I was on the verge of tears, and he sat next to me, putting his arm around me. "Come lay with me," he said in a sweet tone.

I put my head on his chest and tried to pretend like I wasn't still upset. He sighed and said "I just don't know how to deal with you sometimes. I've never argued this much with a girl, ever. Not even Amanda, and we argued a lot." I kept my head on his chest as I re-played what he had said. After a long moment of silence, he said in a joking tone "sometimes I think about just cutting your boobs off and putting them on my wall so I can still have them without any arguing." I looked at him scrunched my forehead like I do when I'm confused and tried to figure out if he was joking or not. He laughed and kissed me, and we cuddled for the rest of the night. I analyzed our conversation as his arms were around me. I was intimidated by his past. He had been with so many girls, and I didn't know how to be a girlfriend. I prayed that I was better than all the girls he was with before me.

On the way back to my house from Collin's with him and Chase, I got a comforting text and my face lit up. It had been a rough couple of weeks for me at school, and it gave me some encouragement to hear from an old friend. Brent and I had been childhood friends. Our dads were friends and scheduled play dates often. We kept in touch growing up, but became incredibly close in 8th grade. We talked on the phone every night and saw each other every day. He was my best guy friend, and he probably knew more about me than even April. I hadn't been talking to him as much since I started dating Collin, but we still updated each other on life every couple of weeks. I was just happy that someone was still there for me and wanting to know how I was doing. Collin noticed my excitement and quickly questioned who I was talking to. I had talked about Brent before, so I didn't think Collin would have a problem with me talking to him. He knew we had been close for a while.

"You don't need to be texting him," he told me.

I quickly snapped back. "Brent is my friend and I'm going to talk to him."

"I said no" he told me; it was the first time he had ever actually told me "no". He was stern and his voice got louder. We pulled up at the curb in front of my house. I raised my voice to match his. "You're not going to tell me who I can and can't talk to. Brent has been my friend way longer than I've even known you and I'm not going to stop talking to him."

I got out of his truck and slammed the truck door behind me and headed for my front door. He got out as well, yelling at me to come back to him - that I couldn't walk away from him while he was talking to me. I kept walking and felt him pull me back by my arm. I tried to yank away, but he grabbed my other arm and started shaking me. I couldn't make out what he was saying. All I knew is that I was terrified. Chase stayed out of our argument as long as he could, but he pulled Collin away from me. He stared back at me the entire way to his truck. I walked backwards sheepishly. His fists were still clenched and his face was red. His eyes were cold and fierce. Collin sped off in his truck and left me scared and confused in the cold night air. I slipped through my front door without my mom seeing me and ran to my bedroom as quickly as I could. I got in bed and evaluated everything that had happened. I made excuses for him and told myself that he hadn't actually hurt me, so it wasn't that bad. I understood why he didn't want me to talk to Brent. We had a strong bond that would intimidate even the most secure of guys. I thought that maybe it was my fault and I shouldn't talk to other guys. I went back and forth, being mad at him and then at myself. I went to sleep with teary eyes and my phone on loud right next to my head just in case he decided to call me.

I woke up the next morning with no new notifications. I was hoping he would text me to apologize or at least explain himself. The longer the silence went on, the more I believed that I had done something wrong. I thought if he wasn't texting me, I should be texting him. I stood my ground, though, and reassured myself that he would talk to me if he thought what we had was worth saving. Despite his lack of effort and the handprint marks around my arms he had left, I thought had invested too much into our relationship to give up.

He finally caved and asked me to come over to talk. When I got to his house, he sat me down on the couch, begging me for another chance. He apologized and told me that he was intimidated by the relationship me and Brent had and got jealous when Brent's text made me smile. I tried to look at the situation from his perspective, and I understood how he felt. I didn't want to lose Brent as a friend, but I was afraid that may set him off again. I asked what I could do make him feel more secure, reminding him that I was his girlfriend, not anyone else's. He asked me to stop talking to Brent and to delete his number for extra reassurance. I reluctantly deleted Brent's number from my phone, instantly regretting even going to Collin's house. I was torn. I had fallen in love with Collin and I didn't want to let him go. I also wanted my life to stay the same – just with him in it. I couldn't have both. I asked myself if he was worth the sacrifice, and struggled with the question for a while.

I went to tumbling practice with a lot on my mind. I imagined what would happen if I tried to break things off with Collin and start over with a new slate. I didn't know if I could get my old friends back, or if I even wanted to. I had no idea where my life would take me, and that almost scared me more than staying with Collin. I knew that what we had in the beginning was incredible, and I was holding onto the possibility that I could have that again. At school, Collin was all I had. A group of girls started walking behind me every day saying "everyone look, it's Sharpie Girl! She's such a slut". I dreaded walking from class to class more every day. I stood alone in the hallways encountering stares and laughter from girls around me. I saw guys whisper to each other and girls laugh loudly every time they passed me in the hallway. I grew more paranoid by the minute – I thought all of those stares and whispers just had to be about me. I came back to reality as my tumbling coach signaled for me to go. I found it very difficult to focus when it was my turn to throw my tumbling pass. I fell completely on my head, hurting myself pretty badly and making it even more difficult to continue practice. I tried a second and a third time, all with the same outcome. I took a few minutes to catch my breath and unsuccessfully tried a few more times. I left before class was over. I called my mom to come get me, trying not to cry. In that moment I realized that I even lost cheerleading. It felt as if my life was spiraling out of my control. Collin was the only thing that I felt was constant. I leaned on him more while be crushed everything in my life without me even being aware of it.

I hadn't talked to Brent since Collin made me delete his number. I checked my phone in class and recognized Brent's number. I resaved it and read his text – "Hey, I just wanted to let you know that Collin is the one who told everyone about the whole Sharpie thing. He showed it to all of the guys in the locker room the day after it happened. I had been trying to get to the bottom of it for you and it was him." I reread the text three times to make sure I hadn't misread. I put my phone back in my purse and took in a deep breath. I couldn't believe that the one person that I trusted, of all people, would be the one person to destroy my reputation. "I'm coming over after school," I texted Collin when I got the chance. I couldn't talk to him about it over text messaging. I had to see his reaction in person.

I got to Collin's house and acted as normal as possible, but I couldn't completely hide my anger toward him. He was already in a bad mood when I got there. He and Chase had been arguing about something. I walked in pissed off, which didn't make his mood any better. I sat down on the couch with my arms crossed and my head tilted, waiting for the moment to confront him. Chase and Collin stopped their argument for the time being. Collin looked at me. "And what are you all pissy about?"

"I'm 'pissy' about you ruining my life."

"You're so dramatic," he taunted.

"I have every right to hate you right now."

"And what could I have possibly done to make *you* hate *me?*" The arrogance in his voice pushed me over the edge.

I started yelling. "You showed all of the guys in the locker room your dick after I signed it. Do you realize what you did to me? That was a joke and now everyone thinks of me as some…"

He interrupted me. "I knew what would happen."

"Collin, you made everyone hate me."

He raised his voice to match mine. "And no guy is going to want to be with a slut like yourself. All you have is me now," he paused and thought for a second. He started walking toward me, pointing at me, "How did you figure that out?"

I was backing up. "Someone told me."

"It had to have been to be a guy."

"Yeah, it was a guy," I carelessly responded. I reassured myself that this was about him, not me or who told me.

"Who was it?" I told him that it didn't matter – what did was the fact that he was the one who told everyone. He didn't like that. He kept asking me who it was with no response from me, eventually progressing into versions of "you're cheating on me" and "tell me." I smirked at his ridiculousness. He looked like an idiot, turning red and shouting the way he was for no reason. That set him off, though. He grabbed my arms, squeezing too tight while yelling "you think this is funny?" pushing me into the wall. I just looked at him, trying to decide if I should pretend to be tough, or if I allow myself to cry. His eyes were growing cold. He was losing himself again. I tried to squirm away and kick him all at the same time. "Fucking TELL ME," he was screaming now. He lowered his voice. "You've been fucking someone else, haven't you? I knew your pussy had been awfully loose lately. It doesn't fit me like a glove anymore. Who is it?" I was still refusing to answer him as Chase was yelling at Collin to calm down in the background. "WHO IS IT?" He was holding me by my head screaming in my face, shaking me, repeating himself. I still just stared at him with confusion and anger on my face, not knowing how to handle the situation. I had never seen anything so frightening – this didn't even compare to the melt down outside of my house. His grip got tighter, his face grew even more red, and I watched him lose himself, bit by bit.

I closed my eyes and pleaded, "I didn't do anything," starting to cry.

"You didn't do anything? You're probably having sex with the whole basketball team," he shouted as he slammed my head into the wall. Chase was physically getting between us at this point. He finally pulled him off of me and pushed him toward his room. Chase didn't say anything to me for a few minutes. I sat on the couch to process what had just happened, a little shaky. "Come on, I'll take you home." He sounded annoyed, which I didn't understand at the time. We got in his truck and shared a long moment of awkward silence.

"Thanks," I meekly said, "for everything." Chase shook his head a little.

"You're not going to stay with him, are you?"

"I don't know, why?" It was a strange question for Collin's best friend to ask me. I honestly didn't know the answer, though. I loved Collin so much, and I just wanted to erase that awful image of him from my mind. I didn't want to accept the fact that Collin had an anger problem, or the possibility of it ever getting worse.

"You're stupid if you stay with him."

I didn't talk to Collin for four days. I contemplated Chase's remark, and thought that maybe he could be right, or actually, I knew he was right, and I was contemplating in which way I wanted to be stupid. Either way I would come out losing, making me an idiot with either route I chose at that point. On one hand, I had nothing except for him. I had no friends, barely any family, and nobody to trust. He was everything I had. I lost so much and I didn't want to lose him too. Despite all of the negativity, he made me feel alive. He gave me such a rush all of the time. He would go from screaming at me to holding me and kissing me all over in a matter of minutes. I hated the times he was screaming at me and shaking me, but I enjoyed all of the attention I got when he was ready to make it up to me. I hated when he was controlling, telling me what I could and couldn't do, but I enjoyed the fact that somebody cared enough for me to get worked up at even the thought of me with another guy. I thought that I could fix him, and with time, all of our problems would go away. With my second option, I could leave him, but what would life even be after that? I had a new life away from anything or anyone I had ever known. My friends were clearly not much of friends, and I had girls I had never even seen before laughing at me and calling me names. The absolute only person I had there for me had already damaged my reputation that much. He could do even more if I hurt him. He was also the only person I could talk to. If I left him, I would have no one. Not one person would be there for me - that was obvious through everyone's actions already. Nobody wanted to be associated with "Sharpie Girl". I knew I was in a tough place, and I decided to give him some space and give us both some time to cool down before I decided on anything permanently. Although, I was leaning toward completely ending things with him. It helped that I never saw him at school. I avoided hallways that I knew he walked through and went straight to each of my classes. I wanted to hate him for everything that he had done, but I couldn't make myself. Despite everything he did to me, I saw good in him – I saw love and insecurity under all of his rage and possessiveness. I felt pity for him. It was impossible to hate someone that I so desperately wanted to help. I wanted to fix him, and I thought I could be the girl to do it. I knew that I needed to help myself first, though, so I focused on letting him go.

I had been trying to make the best of school cheer practice, especially since I had just quit my competitive team. Everyone on the team was incredibly distant from me, but there wasn't much room for small talk anyway so I focused on what we were learning. At the end of one of our practices, our sponsor sat us down and started talking to us. At the end of all the other practices, she normally just told us to go home and have a good night. This talk was different, though. "So I wanted to let y'all know that being a freshman girl in high school is a scary thing, and being a cheerleader, you're probably getting a lot of attention from senior boys." It didn't take me long to figure out she was talking about me. "It has been brought to my attention that a girl on our team has been acting a little promiscuously. This degrades you and us as a team. You all represent this team, and we need to do everything we can to give us a good reputation. This behavior needs to stop." My face turned red. I was sitting near the front of the circle; I felt like I could feel everyone's stares burning into my back. I didn't smile and say bye to anyone like I normally did. I looked down the entire way to my mom's car, and didn't say a word for the rest of the night. I was absolutely mortified. If I didn't feel alone before, I definitely did when I was called out in front of the whole cheer team. Ignoring Collin was difficult when I needed a shoulder to cry on, and his was the only one available.

Collin finally texted me. It was during school, and I was having as rough of a day as ever. "Hey, I want to talk." I didn't text him back. I got another text an hour later. "Look, I know you're reading these. You always check your phone during class. Just meet me in A hall in the square after school. Please." I wanted to see what he wanted, and I can't deny that I had been missing him, or missing having someone to talk to, at least. I teared up as I agreed to meet him.

Our "A hall" was the main hallway of the school. Near the far left of the school was a square of lockers that nobody used. Instead, it was used for kissing before and after school or between classes. I stared at the clock for the rest of the school day, waiting for the clock to strike three. It was torture. I needed to hear what Collin had to say. I saw him leaned up against a pillar in the square. His eyes were soft again, and he gently smiled at me. I walked up to him with my arms crossed and an annoyed expression on my face. "Yes?" I asked him, in a harsh tone.

"Are you having sex with someone else?"

"Are you kidding me right now? You really asked me to come all the way over here so you could ask me if I'm cheating on you?" He looked at me with an uncomfortable expression. "No, and I can't believe you'd even think that." He reached out to hug me. I looked at his arm and back at him, refusing to let him wrap those strong arms around me. "Come on, McKenzie." I continued to stare at him. He put his arm around me against my will and pulled me close. He squeezed me tightly while he whispered in my ear, "Just come over tonight."

I pushed him off of me. "Why? Why would I want to see you?" He put his hand on my cheek – that soft, gentle hand – I closed my eyes for a second. He kissed my forehead. I became strong again. I slapped his hand and started to walk away. He walked next to me. I walked faster.

"I'm just going to keep following you," he said as he smiled that charming smile. I tried not to look at it.

I stopped in the hallway and turned toward him. "Collin, I deserve more." He looked hurt.

"It was an accident. The past is the past. Let's keep it there." I rolled my eyes and started walking again. "McKenzie, I love you. I don't want to be with anyone else and I couldn't imagine you with another guy. Just come over and let's forget this ever happened."

I ignored Collin until I got to my mom's car. I didn't text him back when he texted me, and I resisted all urges to call him. I had hoped that in our separation, school would get better. Things at school progressively got worse, though. My usual seat at lunch had been filled, leaving me to sit at the end of the table in silence. I didn't know what to do or where to go. I had hoped that all would be forgiven with time and I could have my friends back, but it was proving to be a meaningless objective. I started sitting in the bathroom alone, eating very little or nothing at all, and then returning to class when lunch was over. So many times I considered walking out of the big glass doors into the parking lot and never coming back. I didn't have a car, though, and I would have probably been too scared to leave campus anyway. I would get sent to alternative school if I was caught skipping, and I didn't need anything else to hurt my reputation or my relationship with my mom. Despite my anguish, I did my best to hold my head high.

I still hadn't forgiven Collin for telling everyone about our Sharpie incident. I had been ignoring every message he sent me, but it was getting more difficult every time I saw his name pop up on my screen. I wanted him to stay away from me, but I needed someone on my side. I felt like everyone in the entire school was against me except for him, even though it was his fault. It was a constant internal battle. I felt stuck in a rut, not knowing which direction to take. I felt like life would stand still until I chose a path. My "perfect" life had spiraled down in a matter of months. Collin's response to the criticism was "all we have is each other, babe." That wasn't true for him, though. He still had all of his friends and by his side. It was his fault that everyone knew what I had done and thought I had done much more. While everyone else was calling me stupid and criticizing me, he was telling me that he loved me and wanted me forever; I clung to him. He convinced me that he was all I needed, and I had no trouble believing it. He was everything to me. He was the only one that hadn't turned his back on me when everyone else had. I went back and forth from telling myself that I could fix him and make him better to telling myself that I would only get better if I persevered and stayed away from him in my time of desperation. I decided that it was best to stay in my stagnant state until I separated my logical thoughts from my reckless, irrational feelings.

In the meantime, I tried to make the best of my situation. I reassured myself that school was just that – a place to learn. I had put too much emphasis on my social status. I only had to be there for four years and then I could go anywhere. I focused on my grades and put more effort into my homework. I listened in class and kept my phone put away. I tried to figure out who I was and who I wanted to be. I thought that in solitude that would be easy, but I found it much more difficult than I had expected. All I kept coming back to was the person I was before I got tangled up in Collin. Life after graduation seemed too far away to even dream about. I stopped eating in the bathroom and told myself that I didn't deserve that. I started sitting with a group of girls that were a year older than me and kept to themselves. They seemed to not hold my reputation against me, but I was hesitant to trust them anyway. Anything was better than sitting in the bathroom, though. I made small talk with them until lunch ended and thought that could be enough to keep me content until the year was over. I had a new mentality at school. I didn't need friends; all I needed was to survive. Collin's lunch was after mine, and most of his classes were on the opposite side of the school. Without him around, I felt alone. Despite my advances at lunch, I felt like most of the school hated me. Walking through the hallway between classes was torture, and seeing my old friends move on in life without me was painful. Every whisper I saw and every laugh I heard I assumed was about me. It was mortifying.

While trying to figure out what path I should take, I decided that I should allow myself to be happy. All I kept coming back to was Collin, though. Even if my friends would forgive me, I didn't think that I should forgive them. They left my side when I needed them most and watched as my life fell apart. I couldn't get past that. I knew that the rumors of Collin cheating on me were probably true, but I didn't want to accept it. I felt like Collin was the only person to give me a choice. The love my mom and friends had for me proved conditional; they only would accept me if I was acting according to their idea of perfection. I thought Collin wanted me all the time. He wouldn't stop talking to me no matter how many times I told him I was done. I had been called stupid by almost everyone I knew, including the people that I trusted to support me in confusing times. He was calling me perfect and beautiful, and telling me that he wanted to be better for me. I fell back into his trap, thinking I needed him. Gravitating back toward him was easy. I felt like no matter how strong I tried to be, I would always be fragile. He was building me up, and I didn't want to let him go. I still had hope that I could fix him, and I thought he was the only person that could fix me.

3

GREED

I had pretended to be sick for three days in a row to skip school, and on the fourth day I tried to skip, my mom told me that she enrolled me into a new school. It was a private school in one of the neighboring cities, and I didn't know one person. I grew excited over the next day, and finally got out of bed for the first time in days to pick up my new school uniform. I thought that it could be my fresh start. I wasn't nervous on my first day – I knew that it couldn't possibly be worse than my previous school situation. The first day had gone better than I had even imagined it would, though, and I couldn't wait to tell Collin. I wanted him to know how nice and accepting everyone was, and how much I liked all of my teachers. Nobody knew anything about me. All they knew was that I was new, and that's all they would know. I wouldn't have any judgmental girls laughing at me in the hallway or nasty boys looking at me like I could offer something that they would like. I felt respected for the first time in months. I thought that I could be with Collin and have a good life too, like I had longed after for so long.

My mom picked me up from my first day at my new school and dropped me off at Collin's house. I was so excited to tell him about all of my new friends and how amazing my first day went. I walked into his house with a huge smile on my face and ran up to him with open arms for a big hug. He just stood there, and his face didn't match mine. "You talked to guys," was the first thing that came out of his mouth.

I put my arms down and looked at him with my head tilted. "I mean yeah, of course I did. There are guys at the school and I couldn't be rude."

"You talked to two guys in your first class, you talked to Colton at lunch and in your third class, and you talked to Matt at lunch and in your last class." When he noticed the shocked expression on my face, he continued to tell me, "I'm watching you, always. I always have eyes on you. Don't fuck up and be fucking stupid, McKenzie. I will know. Don't think you got away with anything. Consider this a warning." I was speechless. I knew that I could be a flirt, but I made a conscious effort to stop for Collin, and I thought that I had done a pretty good job.

"Collin I didn't do anything," raising my voice, "I didn't flirt with anybody. I had to respond to everyone who made conversation with me. I would be considered rude if I didn't."

"You were laughing with Colton and telling Matt things about me and you. I think that's a little more than 'responding' when people talk to you," he sternly responded, raising his voice.

As I was about to tell him he was crazy, I got a text message. My phone was on the charger on the ground near him, so he looked at it first. Before he said anything, I knew it must have been from a guy. I saw his fists clench even harder than they already were and his face turn red. He threw my phone on the ground, breaking it in half. He threw one half at me and one half out the door. I looked at the blood rushing down my leg and then at his mom who had just walked in. She told me that I shouldn't have been talking to other boys and told me that she needed to take me home. I was too in shock to cry or argue. I tried to process what happened the entire silent car ride to my house. When she blamed the incident on me, I started to believe that maybe it was actually my fault. I didn't know how bad my shin was until I got home and cleaned it. I wore pants for the next few weeks to cover up my leg and avoid any more questions about bruises on my body.

I told myself that things would get better after I had been at my new school for a little while – he just needed time to adjust. He told me he loved me so much that he was terrified to lose me, and that's why he got so mad when I talked to other guys. He was insecure about me being at a new school with a lot of people he didn't know. I understood, and I did my best to reassure him that I was his. I knew that me moving would be a test of our relationship. In a way, I liked how possessive he was. He told me he was in love with me, and he didn't know how to handle that. He just wanted all of me, all the time. I loved how much he loved me.

I was more hesitant to talk to people at my new school after I knew that someone, or multiple people, maybe, were watching me. I chose my words carefully with everyone I spoke to, and I made an effort to not even look at guys, much less talk to them. I wanted Collin to be happy with me. When I got to his house after attending the second day at my new school, he seemed to be less angry with me. It wasn't quite what I was going for, but it could have been worse. I sat with the same group at lunch that day, but didn't say a word to the guys. Apparently that wasn't good enough. He was still mad that I even sat with guys at the same table. I assured him that I wasn't going anywhere. "I'm in love with you, Collin. I'm yours, remember? I won't screw up, I promise."

"I just know you're a flirt," he told me, "and you look really sexy in that school-girl uniform." He smiled, picked me up, and carried me to his bed. "Can you please take everything off but that skirt?" he excitedly begged. I laughed, and I was happy that he was coming around to the new school idea. He kissed me more than usual that day and held me until I had to go home.

I woke up the next day incredibly in love with Collin. I didn't know it was possible to love someone so much. I made an even stronger effort at school to only talk to girls, not because I had eyes on me, but because I loved Collin and he deserved me to only have eyes for him. I knew that it wasn't possible for me to have feelings for anyone else, but I had to prove that to him. I knew he had trust issues, so I did my best to make him know that I was his and his only. I had just gotten to his house after school and we were sitting on his couch when he asked me if I had talked to any guys that day. He didn't ask in a paranoid tone or in a way that made me feel like he was angry with me. He asked me like he knew the answer, and it would be no. He asked me like he trusted me. It made me think that maybe we were actually getting somewhere.

"No I didn't," I responded, "I wish you would trust me." He kissed me.

"I try to trust you, but with everything Amanda did to me, I have a hard time trusting anyone," he paused, "and you're so fucking hot. I know other guys try and it makes me nervous."

"What would make you believe that I'm not going to cheat on you?" I asked.

"I don't know," he said, "I guess if you just had no communication with any guys at all."

"Well guys are everywhere, it's kind of hard to not have any communication with them."

"You want to talk to guys?" he said in his typical paranoid voice. I got annoyed.

"No, that's not what I said. It's just that guys are in the world and I can't ignore them."

"Talking to guys is a choice, and I can't trust you until you make that choice," he said sternly.

"So what do you want me to do, Collin? Delete all of the guys' numbers in my phone?" I asked sarcastically.

"Yeah that would be a good start." I looked at him with an annoyed expression, but listened to him. My relationship with him was more important than to have those numbers in my phone. I didn't need to talk to those guys anyway, and that's exactly what I was trying to prove to him. After I went through my phone and deleted every guy's number that was saved in it, I hugged him, and he squeezed me tightly. I did what I could to make him happy. I distanced myself from every guy possible, and it was easy except for health class. Colton constantly talked to me, but it never got personal. We only made jokes back and forth during our awkward health lectures. It made the time pass quicker for both of us. Colton's pregnant girlfriend, Emily, was incredibly jealous. I would occasionally see her look in the window of our classroom. She was checking in on him. Most of the time, we were talking discreetly enough so that it wouldn't be obvious to the teacher that we were making fun of almost everything she said. That meant that it wouldn't be obvious to Emily that we were talking either. One day after a few weeks of joking around, the teacher finished a little early and let us have the rest of the class period to talk. Colton was completely turned around in his desk talking to me and I was laughing. I saw Emily look in, and we made eye contact. Colton turned and looked at her as she stomped away. "Oh no," he said.

"What?" I asked, "we were just talking." Without saying anything else to me, he asked the teacher for a bathroom pass. He hustled out of the room and didn't come back until the bell rang. I was annoyed for the rest of the school day until I got to Collin's house. I thought he would make my day better; he always did. I resisted telling him what had happened. I knew he would take it the wrong way. He was weirdly distant from me when I got to his house. He barely talked to me and seemed annoyed with me every time I spoke. "You should just get your mom to come get you. I'm going out with my friends," he told me. I listened. I wasn't going to stay somewhere I wasn't wanted. Collin didn't text me the entire night, so I went to bed a little hurt. I didn't want to start a fight over nothing – we had been doing so well. I didn't want to seem like that clingy girlfriend that nobody wants to be around. I thought maybe I was being a little paranoid and there was nothing wrong with wanting a night with his friends. I went to bed telling myself that everything was okay.

The next day I gave Collin his space. I went about my day as normal as I could, besides checking my phone every chance I got to see if he had texted me. He hadn't. Lunch time came around and we all noticed that two people were missing from the table – Emily and Colton.

Everyone asked back and forth where they could be and exchanged their theories. I sat in silence. I didn't know quite where they were, but I knew exactly why they weren't sitting with us. I got to health class and wanted to ask Colton what the deal was. I thought maybe I could offer to talk to Emily and let her know that I had a boyfriend, that I respected their relationship, and that we were just friends. I held my breath. He looked at me and looked away. He clearly didn't want to talk. Emily walked by two times during the class period and happily smiled each time when she saw that he was paying absolutely no attention to me. It happened – I was an outcast at the new school too, I thought. I knew it was only a matter of time before everyone hated me there as well. I did my best to brush it off and went home. I finally texted Collin and asked him if he wanted me to come over. He responded with a simple yes, and I hurried over. When I got to his apartment and walked inside, he didn't seem at all thrilled to see me. "So I know that you've been flirting with Colton," he said, "Emily told me."

I stood in silence. She was the spy. "Why is everything I do blown up so much out of proportion?" I asked, "Collin, I wasn't flirting with him. We just joke around in health class. It's an awkward class and it makes the class go by faster."

"I can't have you joking around with other guys," he smiled as he went on, "you want to see what I've been saying to Emily to get you back?"

"Yeah Collin, go for it," I sarcastically and dreadfully agreed. He pulled up his Facebook messages and brought up a long conversation from her. I noticed that they had been talking all day, when he somehow didn't have the time to talk to me. He scrolled down and what I read stung. "I'm going to fuck you so hard that I'm going to hit your baby's head with my dick," he told her. I looked at him with tears in my eyes. I had never confronted him with the rumors after April telling me he cheated on me at our competition, even though I knew deep down that they were all true. I didn't want them to be true, but I finally admitted to myself that they were. This wasn't some one time accident, either. He deliberately tried to hurt me. There wasn't much I could do, though. To him, I had "cheated" first, somehow.

"I'm just getting you back, McKenzie. You hurt me first. I can't let you get away with it. And I'm excited. She's fucking hot – way sexier than you." The tears came. I texted my mom to come get me while trying to hold myself together. "What's wrong? You can't handle the truth?"

"Collin, I don't deserve this. I didn't do anything. You're acting like a douche bag," I said, raising my voice and sobbing.

He stood up and yelled at me, "You deserve nothing. You're a fucking slut." I tried to push past him to leave and he blocked the door. I pushed him over and over again as hard as I could. He eventually grabbed me by the throat, squeezing tightly. I fought for a while and started growing weak. He dropped me and I held my throat as I stumbled outside and sat on the porch, waiting for my mom. "I'm not done with you," he forcefully said as he followed me outside. I ignored him. He grabbed my purse and took each item out of it one by one, as he threw it at the brick wall. "Look at me!" he screamed in my face. I got up and pushed him again and tried to yank my purse out of his hands as I begged for him to stop. He threw my purse on the roof. A lot of my makeup was broken, my brand new bottle of perfume was busted, and my iPod touch was shattered. "You don't like hearing that you look like a fucking duck? Colton would never want you. He wants Emily, because she's hot. You have a flappy pussy. Your pussy lips fucking blow in the wind. No guy is ever going to want you."

"Fuck you," I forcefully responded as I gathered my things and climbed the fence to pull myself on the roof to get my purse.

"You're a joke," he said laughing as he walked inside.

I gathered my stuff and my thoughts while I waited for my mom. The tears had stopped and I acted as normally as possible, but she knew something was wrong. The overwhelming smell of my perfume and me waiting for her outside of the apartment signaled the fact that something bad had happened. "Did he hurt you?" she asked. I was as vague as possible, and showed her my broken belongings. "We need to go to the police," she tried to persuade me. I didn't want Collin to be mad at me, but I didn't want to jeopardize my relationship with my mom. "I'll think about it," I told her.

I confided in Brent. I wasn't sure if he would even want to talk to me, but I needed him. "Brent, I know I haven't been a very good friend lately, but can I talk to you about something?" He sounded worried. "Yeah, anything." I knew he would never turn his back on me. "My mom is trying to get me to press charges on Collin," I told him in a hesitant voice. "Why?" I tried to avoid telling him, or anyone for that matter, what Collin did to me. "He kind of lost it today, and he broke some of my stuff." "McKenzie, tell me everything." He was getting angrier with every bit I told him. He took a deep breath, cooling down a bit. "You need to press charges. He doesn't deserve to be able to get away with doing that to you." "You're right," I told him. "If you need anything else, please let me know." I thanked him. He told me it was going to be okay, and told me I should be with someone else, someone better. He was the only person to even remotely convince me that I deserved better. At some point every time we talked, we would plan our getaway to California. He was going to be a rock star and I was going to be a movie star. We would go together and never look back. I always counted on that, even while I was with Collin. It was no wonder why Collin hated him so much. I loved Brent deep down, which was obvious to everyone but me. I was just always with someone else. He comforted me and told me that he would come over if I needed him.

As I got off of the phone with Brent, I heard guitar playing from outside my window. I walked outside to see Jordan, a guy that lived a street over, and his friend Kevin, in the cul-de-sac of my street. I had met them when I first moved into that house from across town. I had spent many sleepless nights just sitting in the street and listening to Jordan play the guitar and Kevin sing. That all stopped when I started dating Collin, though. I hadn't even talked to either of them in weeks, so I awkwardly just sat down with them without saying any words. Eventually I had revealed to them what had happened. They were both wanting to kill Collin after I told them, but they settled for me going to the police station. With Jordan, Kevin and my mom, I felt a little better about going. I still felt vulnerable. I felt like Collin would find out and would do something to me or them. I was scared, but I trusted everyone else that going to the police was the right decision.

We had to go to the city police department in which the incident happened. The odds were against me when a family friend of Collin, out of probably eighty or so officers for that city, was the one to take my case. Kevin, Jordan, and my mom quietly sat back and listened as I told him what had happened. "We both know that I personally know Collin, but I want to assure you that I won't let that affect this. I know how he is and I am going to handle this professionally," he promised me. He took pictures of the bruises on my neck and arms and all of my broken possessions, and promised that he would get back with us as soon as he had the chance. As it turns out, he never filed my case. Collin called me the next morning.

"You're a dumb bitch, you know that?" I was silent. I knew he had found out about me going to the police station. "You really didn't think that he would tell me y'all went and tried to press charges on me?"

"No, Collin, I didn't think he would tell you. But I had to go. You broke all of my stuff."

"And you were being a slut. You cheated on me. You're lucky that's all I broke. I know you brought two guys with you."

"For the last time, I didn't cheat on you." I raised my voice.

He ignored me, and he sounded defeated. "I can't believe you did that to me, McKenzie, we just got in a fight. Y'all tried to get me put in jail for statutory rape. I would never do anything like that to you. You could've ruined my life."

"What? I didn't try … Collin I'm sorry, my mom must have tried to do that without me knowing. I would never want you to go to jail over something we both consented to." My mom lost my trust. She finally had gotten somewhere with me, and she went behind my back.

"Well I think it's really fucked up, what you did. I was going to ask you to come over today so we could make up, but never mind." His tone was defensive again.

"My mom talked me into going. I didn't even want to."

"I just really can't believe you would even do that behind my back." Somehow things got completely turned around to be my fault in an instant. I felt so bad for hurting him. I knew he would hate me for what my mom tried to do, and it was something that I would never even think about doing to him. I wanted to prove to him that I was loyal and would never do anything bad to him. I wanted to be that girl for him that would change things – make him that committed guy that fell in love with the perfect girl, and nothing else mattered – I failed. I wanted to do everything I could to make him know that I could be that girl if he gave me another chance.

I didn't talk to Collin for a few days, but I had started to miss him. Still, I was resisting the urge to call him. I knew I didn't deserve what he did to me, and I didn't want to put myself back in that position. He stopped trying to turn things on me when he saw that it wasn't going to get me to come back to him. Instead, he started begging me to take him back constantly, telling me he was sorry and that he just needed one more chance. Over and over again he swore that he loved me and couldn't live without me. They started out as texts, and then progressed to calls. The calls got more and more desperate as time went on. I couldn't keep ignoring him. I had to respond, and in the beginning I was politely telling him to leave me alone, but I was having a difficult time rejecting him for two reasons. One reason was that I undeniably missed him and uncontrollably loved him. My body ached for him. I was upset because of things that he had done, but he was the only person that I wanted to console me. e was the only person that could. All I wanted was to be in his arms, but it was because of his own doing that I even needed someone to hold me in the first place. For that, I hated him, which brings me to reason two. I wanted nothing to do with him. His constant begging had become plain annoying. I wanted to yell at him for everything he had done to me. I couldn't find the words, though. I didn't know what I was supposed to say. He acted like me leaving him was some irrational choice that I had made but he apologized anyway to "be the bigger person," and all I had to do was to come back and everything between us would be fine. His nonchalant behavior about him being so rough with me made me think that his behavior was normal or acceptable. It probably was acceptable in his eyes, but at the time, I didn't see him as something different than the typical person with logic and reasoning. He had such deep and extreme emotions. Everything about him was so intense. When he was happy, he was so passionate about life and me. He held me so tightly and kissed me in a way that I couldn't explain. I never doubted his love for me while he was kissing me. It may have been the way he lightly touched me, or the way he never wanted to stop, but it made me forget every other bad thing about him. As he was calling me, I would think about those kisses. I would think about all of the good, and I had to protect myself from falling again. I turned from polite to plain rude as he called me, and it killed me to hear pain in his voice. "Please McKenzie, please just come see me. I'm sorry. I just want to hold you," he begged in a desperate tone. "I don't deserve what you did to me, and you definitely don't deserve me. I can get someone who won't tell other girls he wants to have sex with them," I sharply replied. That hurt him even more. "I know you can," he said, starting to get a little choked up, "I don't want you to, though." "Then you shouldn't have talked to her," I responded with no remorse, although it hurt me to say it probably as much as it hurt for him to hear it. Our conversations were typically the same each time he called, and I would normally just hang up on him after a few seconds of silence. This time, though, there wasn't silence.

"If you hang up on me again, I'm going to kill myself," he said in the most serious tone.

"No you're not," I said, unsure of its truth.

"Yes I will. I just want you so much. Please come see me," he said.

"I can't come see you and you know why."

"Please just come. I'm sorry," he was definitely crying now. I didn't know what to say. I was speechless, and he just kept begging.

"I can't be with you, Collin," I finally responded.

"Then let's just end things in person. I at least need closure. You can at least give me that." I agreed, though I dreaded him coming to my house. Ending things would be harder in person, and he knew that. He got to my house ten minutes later, and I walked out and sat in his truck in my driveway.

"You know, this is where we first fell in love," he said smiling. I just nodded my head. I wasn't going to let him get to me. "Look, I know I messed up, and I'm sorry. I'll let you say your goodbyes and be on my way," he said. I was a little confused at this. I figured that he'd put up more of a fight considering how desperately he had been trying to get me back.

"Fine, bye," I said, opening the door to get out of his truck. He grabbed me by the arm.

"That's all you have to say to me after everything we've been through?" I just looked at him. He was starting to tear up, which made me start to tear up.

"I have some things I want to say to you," he said, "I am truly sorry. I haven't been a good boyfriend to you, and I'm going to work on that for the next girl I'm with." That caught me off guard. I didn't even fully process anything else he said. I was focused on the "next girl" part. I didn't want there to be a next girl. I kept picturing his perfect lips on another girl, and I instantly got jealous. He continued with something like "I want the next guy you're with to be everything you deserve...everything I couldn't be for you. I love you and I really hope you're happy and this is what you want." I was still on the "next girl" issue. He was mine – not some other girl's. I didn't want that to change. I started to cry. He reached out and hugged me. I put my head on his chest, not knowing what to do.

"We don't have to break up, McKenzie," he said, "you're choosing this. You still have a choice."

I kept my head on my shoulder as I said, "You hurt me, Collin. I can't be hurt like that."

"I know," he responded, "but do you love me?"

"Yes, I do." I couldn't lie.

"Then just give me another chance. Just trust me. I don't want to come this close to losing you again." My brain told me to run fast and never look back. Collin had become the death of me. My heart, though, told me that Collin had given me life. My heart told me to stay in his arms for as long as he'd let me, and never let go of something so real. I decided to follow my heart.

My mom had been hostile and was rude to Collin when she saw him. I longed for her guidance, but the approach she took left me feeling alone. I started to miss my dad, and that only increased every time my mom wasn't emotionally there for me. After my parents got a divorce, I stayed with my mom. I didn't talk to my dad at all. I was 11 years old – that's a delicate time in a girl's life. Since my dad was the one to move out of the house, I blamed him for leaving. My mom made subtle comments about how I shouldn't see him and how the divorce was all his fault. When I had gotten a little older, I didn't care whose fault the divorce was. He was my dad, and I wanted a relationship with him. I loved him, of course, and I was rejecting him from my life. I wanted so badly to just call him, but it had been too long for a simple phone call to mend our relationship. I had never told anyone about this. I guess I was embarrassed or ashamed for pushing him away and maybe even for him being gone in the first place. I hadn't told anyone about my dad, but Collin got me to talk about him. He touched me in a way that nobody else had. He somehow pulled all of my stubborn feelings and memories out of me that don't want to come out for anyone. I showed him the vulnerable side of myself that I have never been able to show to anyone else. He comforted me and told me that it would be a good idea to call my dad. He told me that he would be there for me every step of the way, and he was. I called my dad the next day with Collin holding my hand. We agreed to meet at Texas Roadhouse that weekend.

I was hesitant to walk in, but Collin hugged me and told me that it would be fine. He squeezed my hand when I saw my dad sitting at a table waiting for us. My fears all went away when I saw how excited my dad was to see me. I hated myself for leaving him out of my life for so long, and I loved Collin for pushing me to let my dad back in. I told my dad about how my mom had been trying to get me to leave Collin. He told me that we were always welcome at his house. Not only did I get my dad back that night, but I got another place to see Collin. My dad was going to be happy for whatever I wanted at that point in time. He wasn't going to let me slip away again.

After we left the restaurant, Collin and I were both excited to have another location to meet up. My mom thought we broke up, and letting her believe that was easier than telling her the truth. His mom wasn't a big fan of me either. He didn't come to my house at all and I only went to his when we knew there was no chance she would come home. I was still hesitant to actually go to my dad's house, though. I needed to take it one step at a time. Collin's mom called him and told him that she would be sleeping at her girlfriend's house, so we knew that it would be safe for me to go over there for the night. Collin parked far enough down the street for his truck to not be visible from my house when he brought me to get some clothes. I told my mom that I was going to April's for the night, and walked back down the street for Collin to pick me up without my mom seeing his truck. That's when the lying began.

4

ANGER

Collin and I had been doing really well since he told me that he would try to be a good boyfriend for me. Some of the things that Collin did, though, contradicted his promise to me and what I longed for him to be. I wanted him to be the sweet guy that asked me to be his girlfriend on his tailgate, the guy that put his hand in my hair and kissed me, making me feel like nothing else in the world mattered. The guy that I had met back in January, though, had slowly disappeared. I questioned our relationship often, but he always knew how to keep me close. He sang "I'll Be" by Edwin McCain, putting his hand on my face singing "tell me that we belong together" and "I'll be better when I'm older." The way he so innocently stared into my eyes when he sang those words made me hold onto the promises of the past. If what he was singing was actually true and he could be better when he was older, I couldn't give up on him.

My mom never liked Collin, even before she tried to get me to press charges on him. She had always suspected that there was something wrong with him. I never had a personal relationship with my mom, and I resented her negativity toward everything I liked. Every time I got excited about something, she would shoot it down. My ideas and plans for life were all too irrational, too risky for her liking. I began to distrust her feelings and opinions. She never taught me to take chances, but to play it safe. I thought safe was boring. Collin wasn't safe. Me and my mom both knew that, but I viewed it differently than she did. I saw being with him as living, not just being alive. I wanted every aspect of my life to be extraordinary, and being with him was the only way I knew how to do that.

Daily, I told my mom that I was walking to April's house and I would get picked up by Collin at the end of my street. She seemed to be excited that I had been spending so much time with April and staying away from Collin. One night my mom caught me getting out of his truck at the end of my road. The guilt was overwhelming, although I acted defensive. I told her that if she could just be accepting of my decisions, I wouldn't have to lie to her. She blocked his number from my phone and grounded me. Our only communication was through a texting app on my iPad and through Facebook messenger. I wasn't allowed to leave the house until further notice. I called my dad crying, knowing that he would take my side. My dad's house was the one place my mom couldn't stop me from going to. He picked me up the next day for dinner and gave me a new phone on his plan so I could talk to Collin as long as I promised to not tell my mom. I kept that promise for a while, and let her believe she was winning.

I found out that Collin had been doing steroids for the past couple of months. His friends brought it up around me, unaware that I didn't know. That explained the increase in his sudden outbursts and physical aggression. Collin had been picking me up from my dad's house and bringing me to his apartment. While I normally would have liked the privacy, I had been getting scared of being alone with him. The smallest things had been making him mad, and once he was mad, it was like a switch was flipped. He gradually had gotten more violent with me. Once I accepted a little yelling, it was easier to accept when he squeezed my arms and yelled in my face. Once that had been happening for a while, him grabbing me by the arms and shaking me didn't seem to be that big of a deal. It all happened so slowly that I was desensitized to it. It wasn't until he actually hurt me that I started to fear for my life.

We were on the couch when we started to talk about how much he had cheated on me. Our conversation developed into a heated discussion, and I ended up on the floor with his hand around my neck. He quickly took it off, realizing what he had done. He apologized quickly, but that didn't take away how scared I was. I solely blamed the steroids. I thought that I could convince him to stop doing them, and that he would go back to being sweet and harmless. I stopped going to his house and made him come to my dad's house instead. I felt safe there with my dad and I enjoyed the bonding time. I completely convinced myself that it was all temporary.

I made excuses for everything Collin did to me. I told myself that the cheating was my fault and could be fixed if I gave him what he wanted, and rage was just a side effect. What I felt for Collin was something I had never felt before. I thought I was completely in love with him. I didn't want to be a quitter – I didn't want to give up on what we had in the beginning. I had always been told that love would conquer all, so I had no reason to believe that with my patience and unconditional love, Collin wouldn't get better. As time went on, I began to wonder if love was strong enough to conquer anything, or if it even existed at all. At the time, the line between love and what I had with Collin was blurred. Lust, lies, and deceit can be perceived as love when you're fifteen and dating the senior boy who tells you everything you want to hear. These things conquered nothing but me, pulling me down more quickly than I wanted to realize. I ignored the negativity and pushed back in my mind the fact that Collin was still cheating on me. At fifteen, I believed I had put too much time, energy, and effort into our relationship to accept it was all for nothing.

I went to my dad's house so Collin could come over, but he made excuses every time I asked him where he was. He eventually stopped texting back at all. I was sitting in my bedroom with no friends and no plans. I shifted positions on my bed for hours, staring at my phone and hoping that he would call. Eventually, I got out of bed and gained the courage to call him, myself. I instantly regretted it when he answered and I heard a girl laughing and telling Collin to come back. I knew exactly who is was when I heard the laugh, and I hated this girl. She was living the life I was supposed to live. She was a blonde cheerleader who everyone loved, and most of all, she was April's new best friend. She had taken that spot from me when I chose Collin. Now she was with him. I hated her. A million thoughts crossed my mind. I told myself that everything was okay – that I was paranoid and that Collin wouldn't do anything to hurt me. I was unable to convince myself.

"What are you doing?" I worriedly asked him.

Half talking to me while paying attention to her, he said, "I'm at a party." I heard him say her name and tell her to go do something. I wasn't quite sure what. He had pulled the phone away from his mouth, but I had heard enough.

"Why are you with her?" I asked, hoping that he would give me some sort of logical explanation.

"I have to go," he said as he quickly hung up on me. I called him back after gathering my thoughts. "What do you want?" he asked me.

"Collin, I thought you were coming to see me tonight," I pleaded.

"Yeah well I decided to come to a party instead."

"Why are you with her?" I nervously asked again.

I heard him say something else to her before telling me he had to go. I threw my phone across the room. I pictured them together over and over again and cried until I fell asleep.

I woke up with sore eyes and a headache, but the sun was shining and I could smell breakfast being cooked. I walked out of my room and sat in the kitchen with my dad. Me staying the night had made him so happy that I almost forgot how upset I was about Collin. I spent the rest of the weekend bonding with my dad and ignoring Collin's texts.

I was excited to go to prom when Collin asked me to go with him, but now it was one week away and I couldn't have been dreading it more. I had started to see the end of our relationship coming, and I was particularly mad at him for ditching me to go to a party with another girl. I had no intention of going to prom with him or forgiving him at all. I didn't know if he cheated on me, but if the past was any indication of how things would play out, I would hear about them together soon enough. I intended to ignore him until I could figure out how to end things with him officially, but he showed up at my house with Jeremy. I wouldn't come outside to talk to him, so he drove in circles on my street and yelled that he wasn't leaving until I finally gave in and went downstairs. Not only did I not want to go to prom with him after everything we had been through, but I didn't think the invitation still stood. Neither of us had brought up the topic at all. I argued that I wasn't going until he drove away. I thought I had won the battle, but when I got back inside, my phone rang. His mom called me and told me that since I said yes when he asked me, it was my obligation to go with him. I began to feel guilty – I knew he wouldn't be able to find another date in such short time, and I had agreed to go. I reluctantly told him I would uphold my original agreement after realizing the lack of choice I had in the matter, and after prom I could officially end things with him.

My mom didn't support the idea, but she agreed that going was the right thing to do. She took me to buy a dress the next day. I wanted to be excited to pick out my first prom dress, but all I could think about was every reason I didn't want to go to prom with Collin. I rejected every dress I tried on, not because I didn't like any of them, but because all I wanted to do was hang up the long dresses for his senior prom and pick out a short dress to wear to freshman prom with all of my old classmates. I dreamed of what my life would be like if I could only take back the night I met Collin. High school started so perfectly and spiraled into tragedy all too soon. If I hadn't met him, I would be making plans for prom with friends. Instead, I would be going to prom with a guy who cheated on me and girls who hated me. I tried to keep a positive attitude, though. My attitude would be the only thing I had control over.

The only conversation I had with Collin until prom night was to confirm plans. He picked me up at my mom's house and came inside for pictures. I put on a smile and told myself to take the night one step at a time – it would be over soon and I could try to get back to a normal life. He told me I looked pretty and kissed me on the cheek when I got in his truck. My half-hearted thank you was enough to show him I wasn't in the talking mood. We met Katie and Jeremy at Katie's house and all rode to prom together. I hadn't thought about who all I would actually see at prom. All of the people who watched as I walked through the door with Collin were the same people who tormented me not too long before. My chest felt tight as they all looked at me. Collin held my hand and I felt safe – I knew nobody would say anything to me with him by my side. The stares subsided and I felt like I began to blend in with Collin by my side. Collin and Jeremy walked around socializing with all of their friends as Katie and I sat at a table alone. Jeremy and Collin finally joined us, but talked mainly to each other. After sitting there for a good bit of time without being acknowledged, I asked Collin to dance with me. A slow song had come on, and I had been imagining him spinning me around in my dress since I walked downstairs and saw him waiting for me. I had imagined my first prom as a magical night that I would never forget. I haven't forgotten it, but not because it was magical. He rejected my offer to dance.

"Why?" I asked him.

"I just don't want to," he rudely replied. I should have left it alone, but I kept going.

"Okay well I want to dance and you should bring me."

"I said I don't want to go," he replied.

"Everyone else is dancing. Let's just go, at least for one song."

"Only the nerdy people dance."

"I see a lot of normal people out there dancing. Just take me," I said, starting to get annoyed. He didn't say anything. "Collin, I didn't buy a dress and come out here with you just to sit at a table," I said rudely.

"And I didn't bring you out here to bitch at me," he said even more rudely. I started to tear up and added this to the list of reasons why I hated Collin. We didn't stay at prom long. Collin apologized as we walked out and told me that he wanted to have a good rest of the night with me. I sarcastically smiled at him and kept quiet until my mom picked me up from Katie's house. I shrugged off all of her questions about how the night went. At first she scolded me for the drinking she thought I had done, but she could see that I was hurt so she let me sit in silence for the remainder of the drive home. That night I messaged him and told him that I thought it would be best if we ended our relationship completely. I rejected his many phone calls from Jeremy's phone until I turned my phone off. I felt uneasy with my decision, not knowing how the next part of my life would unfold, or if it was even possible to start a new chapter in my life. Collin was all that my life was, but I wasn't happy.

I kept my distance from Collin, hoping that time apart would be enough to piece my life back together and move on from him. He messaged me several times a day for a week, begging for another chance. I ignored all of his messages, so he called me off a phone with a number I didn't recognize. I answered, and I felt as if my heart skipped a beat when I heard his voice. I did everything in my power to resist his sweet promises. Deep down, I knew the promises were empty and the sweetness would fade once again. I was rude to him with the intention that he wouldn't want to talk to me, but that effort was unsuccessful. He said he knew we were over, but he wanted closure. He threatened to kill himself if I didn't meet him - it wasn't the first time he had told me that, and I was sure that the likelihood of him following through would only increase with every time he said it. I hesitantly agreed, but swore it was for closure only. I wasn't going to fall into the same trap as I had before. He picked me up at my house and we drove around the city for an hour talking about what all went wrong. He blamed everything he had done on his past relationships, swearing that he just got frustrated with me because every past girlfriend made him have trust issues. He said that he wanted to let himself love me – it would just take a little extra time. He pulled his truck into a secluded area behind a few trees and put his hands on my face and begged me again for one last chance. I was afraid to say no – I knew what he was capable of. I also wanted to believe so badly that he was being honest. I analyzed our conversation the entire way back to my house in an attempt to find some indication of honesty on his part. I tried to reassure myself that giving him one last chance was the right thing to do. I forgave him every time he hurt me because I wanted to be the Christian girl that saved him from his past. I loved him unconditionally because I thought that was what I was supposed to do. Our relationship was a constant battle – every time I thought I had pulled him closer to the good side, I would find myself in darkness shortly after.

When Collin parked in my driveway to drop me off, we got pulled over. I thought it was a strange that we got pulled over right as we pulled into my driveway, but I knew it wasn't a coincidence that the cop was a friend of my mom's. He asked me to go inside and I watched him search Collin's truck from my bedroom window. He found a beer can in his glove compartment and arrested him. Another cop pulled up, and I cried as they put Collin in cuffs. I felt powerless. The cop came into my bedroom and told me to sit on my bed. I thought he would comfort me, or give me the little encouragement I needed to leave him. I needed to hear that I was strong enough to leave, or that there is so much more to life than dating the senior boy who thinks you're cute. I needed someone to tell me that I had a choice, and making the choice to leave would be easier than I imagined. Instead, he stood over me and yelled,

"You are so dumb for being with him. You're one of the stupidest girls I have ever met."

I didn't hear anything he said after that. I cried as I said "you don't even know me," but I was crying so hard my words probably weren't recognizable. Not only was it inappropriate for him to be in a teenage girl's bedroom without her parents present, but to yell at a hurt, crying child is despicable. Hate consumed me. I hated the cop for the way he treated me, I hated my mom for putting me in that situation, and I hated everyone who had given up on me. I felt more alone than I had ever felt, and all I could think about was how upset

Collin would be. I went to my dad's house and stayed over as much as possible. Collin got out of jail the next day, and to my surprise, he wasn't mad at me. He said he was just scared and wanted to be with me. Neither of us brought it up ever again, and we held onto each other a little tighter. So many things had almost tore us apart. We fought hard for each other, and we seemed to get stronger after every attempt to separate us. We never were the same, though. I held on for the sake of how hard I had already fought, and he held on every time I tried to leave.

The amount of arguments we had was increasing, as was the level of violence he showed me. His anger led to more destruction as time went on and began to occur without much provocation. It happened so much that being choked didn't scare me anymore – at times, I prayed that he wouldn't stop and my pain would end right there. My head had been slammed into the wall so many times that I was surprised I hadn't blacked out from at least one incident. I didn't think I could handle much more without breaking mentally or physically, whichever came first. He seemed to take pleasure in my pain - once I was hurt, he got to make me better. He knew that hearing about him cheating on me got to me the most. He would slip details about being with other girls into our conversation. I didn't know what I did to deserve any of it. I felt like his personal punching bag rather than his girlfriend.

I wanted to leave him, but I didn't know how. My mom had been hostile and my friends had scattered. I lost count of how many times I heard that I was ugly. According to him, my boobs were too small and my butt was too big. I looked like a duck and my vagina was disgusting. He ingrained in my mind that no matter what I did, I would never be good enough – that nobody would ever love me. He was all that I had left. He told me that he stayed with me because he felt bad for me. The other girls were better than me. They had better bodies, better personalities, and were more fun. I would never measure up. I didn't understand why he would lie to me, and I had so much evidence that he meant everything he said that I believed all of it wholeheartedly. I felt weak, shattered, and alone. I felt like what I had with him was the best I could get in life, and I didn't want to lose that.

5

PRIDE

The unimaginable was happening. I had missed my period for the second month in a row. I was pregnant. I never consistently took my birth control, but we had strong faith in the pull out method. I never thought getting pregnant would happen to me. The first month that I missed my period, I did my best to ignore it. I had been stressed, and I allowed myself to believe that was the explanation for its absence. The second month that went by with no period, I had more trouble convincing myself that it was just stress. I didn't tell anyone. I didn't know who I could tell. I was scared to tell Collin. I wasn't close enough with my mom to tell her. I had lost all of my friends. Despite the person growing inside of me, I had never felt so alone.

I went to the store to buy a pregnancy test and prenatal vitamins, praying that nobody I knew would see me. I got home as fast as I could to take the test with high hopes that it would be negative and it would be a small pregnancy scare that nobody had to ever know about. Deep down I knew I was pregnant, but I dreaded confirming that and having to do something about it. I threw the box under my sink and decided to take it in the morning, giving me one more night before I had to take any kind of action. I took a prenatal vitamin anyway, put the vitamin container in my purse, and headed to Collin's house. We were playing video games with his friends when my phone vibrated in my purse. He went to pull it out to see who was talking to me, but pulled out the prenatal vitamins instead. He just looked at me. Panic covered my face as I told him we needed to talk.

"I'm going to tell all of them anyways so you might as well just tell me now," he responded. I thought he was joking at first. I stood there for a second waiting for him to follow me into his room. When he remained on the couch, I gained the courage I needed to tell him what I didn't even want to believe, myself.

"I missed my period," I said, looking at the ground and hoping he wouldn't make a big deal about it.

He interrupted me with his explanations. "You're always over exaggerating things. You could just be a couple days late. There are a lot of reasons that you…"

I interrupted him, "twice, I've missed it two months in a row." He was speechless. "I'm pregnant." The stares went from me to him. We were all waiting to see what he would do.

He shook his head. "No you're not." I argued with him until I realized that there was no point. He was in denial, and I had to wait for him to accept it. I didn't want to argue too much and then the test end up showing I wasn't actually pregnant. There was no sense in making a big deal out of nothing. He didn't bring it up for the rest of the night, and neither did I. He had told me I was crazy so many times that I started to believe it. I thought about every other explanation as to why I had missed my period twice, and a number of them seemed possible. I had been stressed, I had recently stopped taking my birth control and my hormones could be adjusting, and I hadn't been eating as much, making me slightly underweight. I tried to find some truth in Collin's denial of my claim, praying that he was right.

I bought a pregnancy test when I missed my period the first time, but I was too scared to take it. I knew that when it was confirmed, it would become all too real. I wasn't ready for that. I took the pregnancy test that had now been under my sink for a month right when I woke up the next morning. Waiting for the results was the longest two minutes of my life. I turned the test over and it confirmed my initial instincts. A rush of emotions overwhelmed me. At this point, I knew deep down that Collin wasn't good for me. I just didn't know how to leave him. I was afraid of him while we were together, but I was more afraid of what he would do if I tried to leave. If I had his child, he would have a hold on me forever. Not only was I scared for my life, but I was scared for that child's life. I contemplated telling him I wasn't pregnant after all and just disappearing. On the other hand, I thought that maybe I did exaggerate. I rationalized staying with Collin by reminding myself that he had never actually hit me. He made me believe that what we had was normal, and anything extra was passion. He was always sorry after he hurt me. I believed that if he knew what he did wrong, he could work on it and get better. I had stayed with him through everything else we had been through, and I thought that it had to be for a reason. The cognitive dissonance was overwhelming.

Despite the competing attitudes toward Collin, there was a hint of excitement in me. For a while all I had wanted was someone that would love me and never leave me. Everyone left my side, but a child wouldn't. It would need me. I dreamed of what it would look like and if it was a boy or a girl. I wanted a girl. I was growing, slowly but surely, in my stomach and in my excitement. I looked at names and hoped that Collin would prove me wrong – that he could be a good and loving dad, and even a good and loving husband to me if we made it that far. All I wanted at this point was for him to love me and for us to make it work.

Jeremy sat on Collin's couch with him as I ate everything I could find in his apartment. "Feeding for two, are we?" he asked me, laughing.

I just looked at Collin, who had a mortified expression. "Yeah," I meekly replied. I stopped eating and sat next to Collin. He didn't put his arm back around me when I sat back down and he didn't say one word to me until Jeremy left.

"So you told Jeremy that you are pregnant," Collin hesitantly asked.

"Yeah Collin, I am."

"No you're not," he argued as he were walking out of his front door. In the middle of me arguing back, he turned around and punched me in the stomach as hard as he could. I tried to cover myself as much as possible, but he caught me off guard. I stumbled, catching myself on the couch, and looked at him with a horrified look on my face.

"We can't have that demon-seed running around" was all he had to say to me. I didn't know what to say, what to think, or what to feel – I was devastated and confused.

I was riding in his truck on the way to my house when the most pain-wrenching cramps hit me. I leaned over and held my legs. When we got to my house, I was still in tears and incredibly mad at him as I slammed his truck door and quickly ran to the bathroom in my room. I pulled down my pants to find that I was bleeding, a lot. I knew it wasn't a coincidence. I started crying even harder. I was about to throw my panties away when I noticed something more than blood. There were three sort of chunks that I assumed to be tissue, covered in my blood. It was enough for me to know that I wasn't just crazy. I was pregnant, and I lost the baby. He killed it.

I felt violated and betrayed, like a small piece of me had been ripped away. I wanted to feel needed and loved, and I knew that I was left with nothing once again. I knew that I would always be connected to Collin if I did have his baby, though, and that was a punishment I never wanted to inflict on a child. Even if I did run away and keep him out of our lives, I would never be fully away from him. His child would be a constant reminder of what used to be. He tried to rationalize his actions, but I didn't know what to say to him. I agreed to talk to him in person after gathering my thoughts. For once, I was speechless. We drove around in silence until he pulled over.

"On your 18th birthday, I'll get you pregnant. That will be my present to you," he promised.

I didn't know what to say. I wasn't happy with him. In fact, I had started to hate him. He made me believe that I had nothing else going for me and staying with him was my best shot at happiness. I bought into his lies, staying with him only out of fear that nothing better would come for me. I also didn't want to confirm what everyone else had been saying. I didn't want to admit that I was wrong. I had fought everyone so hard, and I wasn't ready to give up. I thought giving up meant weakness.

It was finally Collin's graduation day. I woke up happier than usual, holding onto what he had told me the first time I went to his house – "if a guy can stay with a girl throughout his senior year and still be with her at the end of summer, they have a really good chance of being together forever." We had been through so much, but we were already halfway there. Forever with Collin was becoming more of a reality. I sat with his dad throughout the ceremony, and he told me how much Collin adored me and told me that he hoped that they would watch me walk across that stage one day. I couldn't even imagine making it that far in high school, but I was excited to see him graduate. I had hoped that this would open a new chapter in his life, and that he would make a change to live better. I thought that if I stood by his side, he would realize that he didn't need to be with other girls.

I contemplated how my life would be if I really did stay with Collin. He already hated the idea of me being at a small school across town, so I knew he wouldn't be comfortable with me going to college. I couldn't imagine how any holiday would run smoothly – my mom hated him and his mom hated me. There would be no room for compromise. I began to feel trapped. I wanted to escape my unfortunate future with Collin, but I didn't know how. However, the obstacles we faced showed me that we would never stop fighting for each other. I feared that I wouldn't ever find anyone else that would fight for me. The more obstacles we faced, the harder we fought to be together, and the harder we fought to be together, the more I thought we loved each other.

My mom stormed into my room after snooping on my Myspace messages and finding out I had been having sex with Collin. She came in my room already yelling. When I yelled back, she pushed me and told me that I needed to move in with my dad. I texted my dad to come get me and started packing my clothes that instant. I already had a suit case with some of my things under my bed ready for the occasion. She tried to pull me out of my room and nearly pushed me down the stairs. When I resisted and tried to go back in my room for my suit case, she punched me in the face three times. I pulled away from her, pushing her off of me, and tried to grab my stuff on the far side of my bed. She grabbed me by the leg and dragged me off. I squirmed until she left me alone. I was packing the rest of the things I needed until a cop walked into my room. He asked if I was trying to run away, and I answered that she told me to leave. I was just following her orders. He told me that I needed to put shoes on and asked me to put my hands behind my back. I had never felt more betrayed, and I had never wanted to be with Collin more just to spite her. My dad pulled up to my mom's house minutes after I had been put in the car. I watched him start to cry and gripe at my mom as the cop car took me away.

I was asked several times what had happened, and when I told the cop, he told me that he had to arrest me because it was my mom that called. I instantly regretted not calling the cops, myself, and having her arrested and humiliated like I was. I saw the cop and the director of the juvenile detention center talking, and I prayed that they would let me go. My prayers were unanswered. I spent three days wondering how long I was going to be there. The other girls told me that it usually took weeks to go to trial for sentencing. I read a lot of books from our library while in my metal cell, trying not to be angry. All of the other girls were comforting and empathetic, and nobody seemed to judge anyone else. Every one of the girls had a story of how they ended up there, some worse than others, but all unfortunate in different ways. Most of the girls had been abused by their parents, and then put in by those same parents that abused them. The girls all shared a bond – they knew that they could all relate to each other in a way that the rest of society couldn't. They told me that they had all been there several times, and they knew they would be seeing me again. Despite my connection to them, I hoped that wouldn't be the case. My name finally got called to leave, and I wondered who was on the other side of the doors. All of the girls wished me the best, as I did for them. When I saw my mom smiling at me, ready to take me home, I wished I could stay a little longer. I would have traded freedom to be with accepting and loving girls that would respect me. I didn't say a word the entire way home, even though I wanted to scream at her and tell her how much I hated her. I called my dad to come get me as soon as I got in the car, and he was waiting in the driveway when we pulled up. I checked my phone to see what all I had missed in my three day absence from society. A few messages from Collin, a couple of spam emails, and a text from my grandpa. "You're a disgrace to this family," it read. It stung to read, but I deleted the message and put him on my mental list of people that were no longer behind me.

My mom was officially out of my life. I hated her. My dad helped me pack what I needed, and I was excited to start a new chapter of my life with him. I couldn't even wait to get settled at my dad's house before calling Collin. My life had turned upside down and I wanted something familiar for me to feel like at least something was normal. He sounded uninterested in seeing me on the phone, so I hung up and tried to adjust to a new life. Deep down, I knew that my new life would be more successful if I left him out of it. He texted me shortly after, though, and I did my best to move on without him. The more I ignored his texts, the more I was able to see why everyone was opposed to me being with him. At the same time, I found it harder to resist him with every desperate message. I had sacrificed so much for him, though, and I thought that had to be for a reason only my heart knew. I couldn't see a life past Collin and sophomore year.

Collin finally came over for the first time since I officially moved into my dad's house. I was trying to tell him all about my three-day incarceration experience, but he was paying more attention to his phone than to me. I asked him who he was texting.

"Nobody," he responded three times until I forced it out of him. "Fine, if you want to know so badly, I'm talking to Amanda."

"Why are you talking to her?" I knew I'd regret asking.

"I got her pregnant." My excitement to see him completely transformed into anger.

"No you didn't." I didn't want to believe it. He pulled up her pictures on Facebook. "There, look at her stomach. She has a bump."

"When did you do this?" I asked him, not that knowing would make it any better, but I had the right to know.

He told me that it happened a couple of months ago when she got in a fight with her boyfriend. She called him because she was upset, and he went to see her to comfort her. It led to sex, and he swore he didn't intend for it to. Feelings of anger and betrayal circled through my whole body. I just stared at him. I wanted comfort from him after everything I had been through. I missed him while we were apart, and I didn't want to be mad at him. I just stared at him.

"Look, I'm sorry. It happened a long time ago, before we were having sex. I'll get rid of it and we can stay together," he said sweetly.

My dad came in asking if we were hungry, interrupting our conversation. I walked out of my room and focused all of my anger toward Amanda – I needed to be able to let Collin comfort me. The anger I had toward Amanda didn't subside easily. I looked at her pictures on Facebook, picturing her and my boyfriend having a baby together. It drove me insane. Collin pointed out the road to her trailer park the first time we went to my dad's house, and wasn't far. I asked my dad's girlfriend to drive through the trailer park on the way to the store, hoping she wouldn't ask me why. I recognized a cat from one of her pictures sitting right next to one of the trailers, and I knew it had to be hers. I tried to move on with our relationship as normal, but all I could do was picture him with her in that trailer.

6

LUST

I prayed tearful, desperate prayers for Collin to love me, for Collin to change. God didn't answer those prayers, and I hated Him for it. I began to have doubts. I couldn't see how He could make me go through all of it without just helping me. I longed for a relationship with God again, I just couldn't find Him anywhere. Collin's dad was a preacher, and when he told me that at the beginning of our relationship, I assumed Collin would be a strong Christian. He talked about church and told me what he believed in.

I looked back at that moment many times, wondering how a man that loved God could slip into such deceitfulness. I casually brought up that conversation about God that we had shared in the past, and he rolled his eyes at me. "Let's just go to church. Let's try it. Relationships need to be built on God," I begged. I was right, but our relationship was already built mainly on alcohol and sex. Nonetheless, I still wanted to at least try to fix us. I didn't know how deep in love I would fall with him until it happened, and I wanted to do whatever it took to make our relationship great. He shrugged to the question, but it was definitely better than refusing.

Collin received a call from his dad a week later, telling him that the youth campus of his church was looking for a drummer. Collin accepted the offer, and I couldn't have been happier for him. Collin started going to practices the next day.

That Sunday at church a girl named Lacey walked up to us and introduced herself to me after me and Collin walked in together. I asked how they knew each other and they told me that they had met at a party a while back. She invited me to sit with her while Collin played, and I accepted. When he went to get ready to play, she asked me how long have we been together. She seemed shocked at my answer, questioning if we had broken up at any time between the start of our relationship and then. I told her no, and stopped myself from analyzing her questions. I didn't need anything taking my attention away from what mattered – Collin playing. He was phenomenal. I was so proud to call myself his girlfriend. The sight of him playing for God made me love him so much more. Lacey gushed about him and kept saying how nice and funny and amazing he was. I thought she was just trying to get on my good side. I agreed with her. I didn't have many friends at the time, so I was excited when she asked me for my number. We began texting constantly and soon became inseparable. My dad dropped me off at her house and I would stay there for days at a time. We had so much fun together – we connected on so many levels – more than I knew at the time.

Things for me and Collin had been looking up for a change, until I opened his phone to send myself a picture of us that we had taken a few days before. His text messages were still up when I unlocked his phone. I wouldn't have thought anything of it if I didn't see a girl's name that I had never heard of before. I opened their texts and sure enough, he had gotten naked pictures from her. I was more confused than anything. I didn't understand why he would do that to me. I gave him everything he wanted, and I didn't see why he would try to get it elsewhere. I took the phone in his room and just showed it to him with a disgusted look on my face. He just looked at it, laughed, and looked away.

"Why do you have this?" I asked in a serious tone.

"It was a dare," he nonchalantly replied.

"I don't care what it is, you shouldn't have this." He snatched his phone from me. "Whatever Collin, I'm done. We're over," I said, only half meaning it. I wanted him to apologize and tell me he wouldn't do it anymore, but he rudely slammed the door behind me. He was mad at me for being mad. I walked out and got my dad to come get me. I felt used, like I wasn't worthy of Collin's respect. No matter how much I tried, I couldn't make him understand that the things he did were hurtful. Everything he did was justified in his mind. My dad told me that I didn't deserve to be treated the way Collin treated me, but he only knew the pieces that I shared with him. I kept my distance from Collin in an effort to find some direction. It constantly took every ounce of self-control in me to not talk to him. After a week of resistance, my strength was running thin. I couldn't hold in my feelings any longer. I had to just get them out somehow. Instead of telling him, I wrote a letter to him that I would never send.

"I miss everything about you. I miss the way you laughed at every little thing I did, I miss the way you slapped my butt when I walked by and how much fun you had play fighting with me when I tried to cover it up, I miss cuddling with you and every little thing constantly leading to sex, I miss coming home to you and looking for new ways to make you happy. I miss your foot massages and you playing with my hair when I didn't feel good, and I miss playing with yours, facing you in bed wrapped up in each other. I miss telling you my every thought, and you genuinely being interested in whatever I had to say. I miss arguing about nothing and then being adult enough to apologize for it. I miss feeling terrified and secure all at the same time, because that's what being in love and taking a leap does to a person. I miss imagining the future with you, from a glamorous wedding to how our kids would turn out. I miss the excitement I felt every time I looked at you, and the spark I felt every time we touched. I know that I could have made you happier. I wish you would give me another chance, but I'm afraid that you would end up breaking my heart more than you have already broken it. I don't think I could take it another time. I miss every piece of you, good and bad. I've been in love with you since I met you, and through everything, that feeling has only gotten stronger. I've tried to hate you, but how can I hate the one person I want forever with? I have every reason to completely cut you out of my life for good, but I can't shake the longing I have for you. Deep down I keep telling myself that this is just some long fight that we are in and you'll come to your senses and stop cheating on me. Part of me wishes this is true, but for the sake of my future, I'm praying that God sends me someone worthy of my time before you decide you want me and only me again."

I held my ground and kept up my silent treatment. I was set on never getting back with him, although I was getting lonely. My dad worked most days, and I didn't have many friends. I was in the shower when I heard my phone make a noise. I reached out of the shower to grab my phone, and I got a lump in my throat as soon as I saw who it was. Amanda, the Amanda that I absolutely despised, messaged me on Facebook. "Hey! I know this is random, but I heard that you and Collin broke up and that you're living right by me now. Do you want to hang out sometime?" The lump in my throat didn't go away. I didn't understand why she would want to see me, but I needed a friend. I messaged her back and agreed, telling her my cell number. We texted back and forth, and she picked me up that night with her friend Heather. I thought they were going to torture me or kill me – or both. I was terrified. She didn't look pregnant, so I didn't know if Collin lied to me, or if he really did get rid of it like he said he would. We went to Sonic, and when we got to Amanda's trailer, I was sure that they were up to something. I thought, maybe she had seen me stalking her trailer a couple of weeks before because I was right – it was the trailer with the cat. I gulped, and jumped out of the car. I didn't say a word almost the entire time I was with them. I was scared to talk. Collin always told me that she was completely insane. Her and Heather made jokes all night and included me in their conversations as much as I would let them. I envied everything about Amanda, but found myself loving her at the same time. We shared a birthday, except she was a year older. We shared a personality, except she was better. She was me, except taller, prettier, funnier, more outgoing, and she knew how to have more fun. She had an amazing boyfriend and I had no one. I was more comfortable as the night went on. We went to Sonic again, and drove around for a while. They finally dropped me off, and I found myself happy at the end of the night. I thought that, maybe, I could get through the breakup. I didn't need him.

I saw Amanda almost every day for the rest of the summer. I hadn't talked to Lacey since the breakup. I had been spending time with my dad and Amanda and all of her friends, and it was a forty minute drive to Lacey's house. I was trying to get into the school Amanda went to. We had gotten really close over the couple of months that we were friends. We would have stayed close if it weren't for Collin. He had been talking to me again, and I resisted telling her. At that point, I was happy without him. There was just a piece of me missing. I didn't want to get back with Collin because I knew she'd hate me for it. He pulled me back in like he always did, though, and I didn't tell her. I just kept my distance and hoped she wouldn't find out.

I called Lacey, and she agreed to let me come over. We were catching each other up with our lives when I told her how great me and Collin had been since we had gotten back together. I expected her to be happy for me, but her smile faded. "I'm sorry, but I kind of did something that you're not going to be happy about. I wasn't going to tell you, but…" she paused. I knew what she was going to say, and my face was turning red. "I had sex with Collin last night."

"You've got to be fucking kidding me," I thought to myself. I didn't say anything. My face was still heating up. I held my tongue. She could tell I was angry.

"He told me you were broken up," she pleaded.

I walked out and called Collin, screaming at him as soon as he answered the phone. "Just let me come explain, please," he begged, "I'll pick you up and bring you to your dad's house." I let him pick me up. He had no trouble finding her house, which pissed me off. I yelled almost the entire way to my dad's house. I started to cool down and let him explain, like he wanted to. "Now what do you have to say for yourself?" I asked in a harsh tone. He laughed sarcastically and shrugged his shoulders. "Why the hell did you tell her we were broken up?" I hoped he'd have a better answer.

"I wanted to have sex with her."

"Why did you even offer to pick me up?" I asked.

"I wanted to see you," he simply replied.

"Then why didn't you just come have sex with me last night then?" I asked, still using my harsh voice.

"It's a far drive," he said with confidence that implied it was a valid excuse in his mind.

"We were going to church and I thought you were becoming one with God. I thought we were actually making progress. I'm giving you everything you want and you cheat on me with my friend. How could you do that to me?" I did my best to hold back my tears. I wanted to be strong and finally have the upper-hand. That didn't last long.

"I was cheating on you with her way before you even knew who she was." My heart sunk. "Remember Valentine's Day? Remember those guys' nights? I was with her. I was fucking the shit out of her, and let me tell you, it has been fucking awesome. She's so tight."

I restated my first question, now with teary eyes and a louder voice. "How can you go play drums every Sunday at church and act the way you do? How can you be worshiping God and cheat on your girlfriend and not even care?"

He laughed, and then got serious. "McKenzie, I am God."

I wrinkled my forehead and raised my eyebrow like I do when I'm confused. "You're stupid" is all I could come up with. I slammed his truck door and stormed inside with the intention of never talking to him again.

7

SLOTH

I was losing faith that Collin had ever even liked me a little. I felt so unloved, so worthless, and I thought that maybe he really hated me. He broke my heart into pieces, and he kept coming back to break it into more. He broke me completely. Instead of being sad, I decided to be mad. Being mad always made it easier to not crave him. Deep down, I had always known that he was at fault for his cheating, and I was finally accepting that I wasn't to blame. I told myself that I did nothing to deserve to be cheated on. Pain, anger, and sadness overwhelmed me every time I thought of him with Lacey. The image of them was on repeat in my mind. I hated them. I wrote another letter that I never planned on sending. Even though it made me feel desperate and pathetic to write what I did, putting my feelings on paper helped.

"You used to love me. You told me that you wanted to get me pregnant so I would have to stay with you forever. You said that you wouldn't let me leave you – I didn't have a choice. You swore that if we broke up, you would sing to me until I changed my mind. I always knew that we would fight, and sometimes things would get really bad, but I never imagined we would end up here. What happened to us both crying and apologizing after fights, swearing that we would never fight again? We couldn't stand the fact that we had hurt each other. There was so much passion, and you loved me desperately. I will never understand what I did to make you lose that love for me. Now you try to hurt me, playing stupid games with me and pushing me to the edge. It's like you're a completely different person. I want to pretend like I don't care about you like you don't care about me, but I still love you to a point that overwhelms me. I know you loved me before, and I would do anything to make you get that feeling back."

In tears, I called Amanda, and she told me I could come over. I got dropped off at her house she said everything I needed to hear. She was the best person to go to for Collin-bashing. Her stories of him proved to me that he would never change. Amanda was also good at Lacey-bashing, but that ended quickly. She didn't want to add fuel to the fire. I wanted to kill Lacey. I hated her with passion I had never felt before. It was something I didn't know I was capable of. Amanda calmed me down through my crazy, rage-filled episode, and suggested that we go to her boyfriend's house.

When we got to Daniel's house, he and his brother had invited a few friends over. A guy named Jake stayed awfully close to me the entire night. I can't deny that it felt good for a guy to be interested in me, but I wanted it to be Collin. He asked me for my number at the end of the night, and letting go of unrealistic dreams of getting back together with Collin, I gave it to him. My confidence took a step in the right direction as I put my number in his phone. I still couldn't get Collin off my mind, though. I wanted him to see me there, smiling with another guy. I knew he'd be jealous, and I wanted, more than anything, to make him suffer. I wanted him to know what it felt like for the person he loved to be in the arms of another. The part of me that was ready to let him go was proud of me for making an attempt to move on, but also disappointed for not being able to keep him off my mind. I thought about Collin constantly, but keeping his name off my lips for an entire night was something new for me.

Jake texted me early the next day. He told me that he normally would wait for a couple of days to text a girl, but he couldn't wait to talk to me. Normally something like that would have made me excited, but it didn't. I couldn't imagine starting a new relationship with a different person. I hated to admit it, but all I wanted was to work things out with Collin. I was so wrapped up in what he was doing, who he was talking to, and why he wasn't fighting for me. He always knew what to say to make me work harder. Other girls were sexy and fun while I was ugly and annoying. These girls received his undivided attention while he was with them, and he still gave them attention while he was with me. He could never put his phone down. He told me that I would always come before the other girls he talked to, but in reality, his "bitches" were his life, and I came second. Deep down I was jealous of them for having what I thought I wanted. I wanted to be the one to change him. I thought that I could make him loyal and trustworthy, forgetting why he ever wanted something so dirty with those girls. I lost myself trying to be his "one and only". Texting Jake back was my only idea to pull me out of the Collin-cycle.

I agreed to go to church with Jake the next evening. He and his friend picked me up from my dad's house, and it felt refreshing to be with some good guys for a change. They were polite, and I appreciated that our first date would be church. That was something I definitely wasn't accustomed to, but desperately needed. I wanted so badly to find God again. I liked Jake. It didn't even remotely compare to how I felt for Collin, but I knew it could get there. He had everything going for him. He was the type of guy that I imagined myself being with before I met Collin.

After the service was over, I noticed several missed calls from my dad. I called him back as soon as I got back to Jake's truck, and we got in a huge fight. The church service had lasted a little longer than we had anticipated, and he was worried when I wasn't answering his phone calls. I hadn't lived with him in four years, so I understood why he felt scared. The phone call was filled with yelling and telling me I couldn't see Jake again, and ended with me in tears. I didn't like fighting with my dad. He had a temper that I had been terrified of since I was a child. I was afraid to go back to his house and have something ruin the relationship we had built. I wanted to get away so I could avoid getting in any more fights with him. I called my mom, and she insisted on coming to get me back. I had mixed feelings, but I agreed. School would be starting soon, and I felt ready to go back to my old high school. Jake dropped me off at my dad's house and I went straight to my room. Jake seemed hesitant to talk to me after he witnessed me fight with my dad, and didn't text me after that night. There was one person who had always been able to comfort me, and that was Brent. He had never let me down despite everything I had ever done to him. I cried more than I talked, and he stayed on the phone with me until I fell asleep, something he hadn't done since I met Collin.

The next day, my mom came to my dad's house to get me and my stuff. I felt relieved to see her. Her house was my home. I wanted back the life where I was comfortable there. She tried extra hard to make me happy. She brought me shopping to get me ready to go back to school. It was exactly what I needed. I felt dirty in my old clothes. Every piece of clothing I had worn around Collin reminded me of him. She tried to get me excited to go back to school. My anxiety was obvious. I imagined that things were much worse than she assumed. I tried to stay hopeful, though, because Brent would be there. Just the thought of him was enough to take my stress away. I thought about reinventing myself. It was a new school year and I wanted to be a new person. I developed a new style, and my mom bought me blonde extensions to match my hair. I felt pretty for the first time in months.

I spent the next couple of weeks by myself at my mom's house. She worked all day, but I enjoyed the alone time. I appreciated feeling safe and being able to relax for the first time in a while. Staying away from Collin was like quitting a drug. I was doing my best to recover, but a small part of me missed him. The more days I stayed away from him, the happier I got and the less I missed him. My relationship with my mom was slowly improving, but I didn't trust her. That was something that had to be earned back. April started talking to me again after I told her that I broke up with Collin. I did my best to stay at home as much as possible, so our plans consisted of sleep overs at my house. I wanted our friendship to be restored to the point of where it was before I met Collin, but it was hopeless. She looked at me differently, and I had trouble being nice to her after she dropped me from her life. She left me in my greatest time of need, and that's not what a friend does. My transition back into my old life wasn't going as smoothly as I had hoped.

The first day of school crept up on me quickly. I put a shield of confidence around myself, but I was in a vulnerable place. I felt alone and scared, like an outsider to a place where I became very comfortable less than a year prior. With every doubt and rush of anxiety, I kept my head held high. I had no intention of showing anyone any weakness.

Collin always worked so hard to get me back. He had this way of making me fall in love with him again after the terrible things he did to me. Every time I got close to him again, it was just a matter of time before he broke my heart. It was an endless cycle that I was desperate to escape. I thought Brent might be able to pull me out. Without him, though, I knew I would be sucked back into the cycle, eventually ending in death. I was glued to Brent as much as I could be, and things started progressing. He kissed me, and I let him. I had a rush of guilt and excitement all mixed into one. I pushed away the guilt and just let it happen. I let his hands touch my waist and I let him pull me closer to him. I loved the gentleness of his kiss, and I let myself enjoy it.

Collin had been messaging me for a few days, begging me to go back to him. He made promises I knew he wouldn't keep. I resisted him for a while, but he stayed on my mind, even when I was with Brent. I was either comparing the two, wishing I was with Collin instead, or telling myself that Brent was what I needed to get away from Collin. Brent was like the guys in the movies. He was sweet, romantic, thoughtful, and perfect for me. Collin gave me such a high, though. I was addicted. I slowly started replying to Collin's messages. I hated myself for it, but at the same time, I couldn't stop myself. I didn't deserve Brent. The more I talked to Collin, the less I talked to Brent. Eventually, I stopped talking to Brent altogether. I gave him no explanation, but he knew why. No amount of apologies would mend our friendship. I was ashamed of what I had done, but I easily tore myself away from what was good. My biggest regret is not being someone Brent deserved. He always loved me and always would, and I broke his heart.

Collin didn't bring up anything from the past when I finally saw him. I had no intention of telling him anything about Brent; he hated him. He had stopped texting me, so I assumed there would be no way of Collin finding anything out anyway. I had deleted our whole conversation and the pictures we took off of my phone. We were sitting on the couch when we both saw my phone light up from across the room. Collin made it a point to check my phone before I did. He "had to know he could trust me." By Collin's reaction, I gathered that it was from Brent.

"Why the HELL are you talking to Brent?" Collin screamed at me. "I started talking to him when we were broken up, no big deal," I said calmly, hoping I could convince him. "No big deal? Really? No big deal? I bet you've been fucking him this whole time we've been together." I knew things were only going to get worse from there. I didn't say anything. "Really how long have you been fucking him behind my back?"

I told him that he was crazy, that I had done nothing wrong. He called me a slut and started going through my phone, looking for evidence of a relationship between me and Brent. He kept pushing me to the ground as I tried to get my phone from him.

"Stop fucking pushing me," I yelled, as I pushed him as hard as I could back, "and give me my phone." He pushed me back harder. "You've been cheating on me the entire time we've been together, and we weren't even together when I was with Brent."

"So you have been fucking him. I knew your pussy was saggier than usual. You're a fucking slut," he yelled. I slapped him in the face as I yelled "fuck you, Collin." His face grew red and his eyes became harsher than I had ever seen. He dropped my phone as he balled his fists and pretended like he was going to hit me in the face. The closest thing to him was a knife. He looked at it, then I looked at it, and I gulped. He picked it up, and I grabbed my phone and ran out of the apartment and slammed the door behind me. Chase had been telling him to calm down from the other side of the room, and darted after Collin as he followed me out. Chase caught up with Collin, and I turned through yards and streets until I was sure he had lost me.

I was frantic. I had never been more scared in my entire life. Each time Collin got angry, I watched his eyes change more. He was a monster that grew bigger every time we had a fight. I didn't know what he would do to me, but I wouldn't underestimate him. I hid in a big patch of bushes not far from his house, but it was far enough and I was hidden well enough to not be found. It was getting dark out and I was still shaking when I heard Chase calling for me. He had been walking the streets, looking for me, but I didn't trust him. I was terrified to go back. "McKenzie, come out. I'll take you home," I heard him yell. I didn't trust him. When I didn't hear Chase calling for me anymore and I was sure that they were done looking for me, I searched my phone for someone to call. I couldn't call my mom or dad. It would open an opportunity for too many questions that I didn't want to answer. There was only one person in my contacts that I knew could drive that wouldn't lecture me. Stephanie was April's brother's girlfriend. I saw her as a sort-of big sister to April. I had burned so many bridges and I trusted few. She was one of those few.

I texted her and asked if she could come get me from his house. She called me right after I sent the text.

She sounded concerned when I answered the phone, asking me if I was alright. I told her I was fine, but she could hear the shakiness in my voice. She asked me what he did to me, and I told her that there was a lot of yelling and that he chased me with a knife. I tried to downplay what had happened. I didn't need any more attention from people at school. She asked me where I was, and I told her that I had just been hiding in some bushes ever since. "Stay there, I'm on my way," she promised. She parked on the street next to Collin's house, like I told her to, and I crawled out of the bushes. Her mom talked to me from the front seat. "If you ever need anything, let us know." "Thank you," I responded. I remained quiet for the rest of the ride home. I thanked them again for coming to get me. I walked in my room, pulled the covers over my face, and cried myself to sleep.

8

GLUTTONY

I was craving companionship. It was companionship in general that I longed for, not necessarily Collin. He was the first person that came to mind, though, and I thought that I needed him. I picked up my phone and had Chase's number on my screen, ready to push send, so I could hopefully get in touch with Collin and just see him. Instead, though, I called Amanda. We hadn't talked since I had gotten back with Collin, and I didn't think she would talk to me after I stumbled back to him. She never judged me, though, and she picked up when I called. Amanda always dropped whatever she was doing to be there for me. I drove to her house 30 minutes away with tears in my eyes and we didn't talk about Collin. Amanda always understood what I was going through. She never questioned me or lectured me – she just let me know that she was there for me whenever I was ready to let go, and she was.

She was getting her stuff together to stay at her boyfriend's house that night, and invited me to stay over there with them. I agreed. I needed to be around people that wouldn't let me call Collin in the night if I got desperate enough. I texted my mom to let her know that I was staying with Amanda that night. She had no objections to anything I did as long as it didn't involve Collin, and she knew that we definitely wouldn't be seeing him together.

We joined Daniel and his brother, Andrew, on the couch playing Call of Duty. They let us take turns shooting and talking on the mic. We had fun, until Amanda and Daniel headed to his room to go to sleep. Andrew and I just looked at each other. I looked away, and he asked me if I was hungry as he got up to go to the kitchen.

"Yeah I guess," I responded, following him. He handed me two bags of chips, a box of cookies, ice cream, and a container of strawberries. We went to his room and stuffed our faces with all of the food. Collin was on my mind, as usual, but I did my best to not bring him up. I wanted to just be done, to just forget and move on with my life. I was doing better than I thought I would, until he asked how I knew Amanda if I lived as far away as I did.

"Well," I thought to myself, still trying to leave Collin out of our conversation, "I lived with my dad for a while out here." I kept looking down, pushing my spoon into my ice cream.

"But how did y'all meet?" He persisted.

"I was dating her ex, and she messaged me after we broke up," I hesitantly told him, still focused on my ice cream. He accepted that answer and didn't seem to put too much thought into it. I sat quietly, searching in my mind for some new subject that didn't involve Collin.

"Wait, Collin? Were you with Collin?" He raised his voice a little.

"Yes," I said, embarrassed that he already knew that I had fallen into the same trap as Amanda did.

"How can you be with someone like him? I know everything he did to Amanda. I know how he cheated on her and dragged her across the yard by her hair, I know that he was really abusive to her."

"It's...complicated." I knew he wouldn't understand.

"Try me." He was able to get me to do the one thing I didn't want to do – talk about Collin. He opened my Collin flood gate.

"Well, he was really nice to me in the beginning. He was very charming and knew all of the right words to say. Then things got a little more...complicated. He started cheating on me and I didn't want to believe it at first, and then I always think it's my fault. Then he started getting more violent. He had been rough with me, but it rapidly grew worse. I had nowhere else to go so I stayed with him." I began to get a little choked up, looking at the ceiling talking more to myself than him. "I will never love anyone as much as I love him. He makes me feel alive. No other person, ever, will even remotely compare." He attentively listened as I compared the good and the bad, the incidents of why I love him and why I hate him all at the same time.

"McKenzie, you're a sweet girl, and you're really pretty. You could find someone else, someone better. You could have anyone you want, and you don't deserve to put yourself through that. He doesn't love you." Andrew meant what he said, and deep down, I knew he was right. It broke my heart. I halfheartedly smiled and kept eating until I went to the couch in his living room to go to sleep.

I tossed and turned for hours, replaying what Andrew said to me - "he doesn't love you." All I wanted to do was prove that statement false. I knew Collin's number and I knew where Andrew put his phone. All I had to do was sneak in his room and take it for a couple of minutes to call him. I got up and tip-toed to his room. I walked in the door and realized how big of an idiot I was for even contemplating that plan. I was walking out when Andrew turned over and said "hey" in a sleepy voice. "I couldn't sleep," I told him. He waved for me to come closer, scooted toward the wall, and then patted the bed for me to get in. I laid down and fell straight asleep.

The next morning, I woke up to an empty bed. Andrew was making breakfast, and Amanda and Daniel still hadn't woken up.

"Thanks for letting me share your bed."

"No problem," he said as he smiled. Amanda and Daniel joined us shortly after, and I felt like a huge weight had been lifted off my shoulders. There really were good guys in the world, and Andrew and Daniel showed me that. Andrew also made me realize that Collin didn't love me, and probably never did. I didn't accept it at the time, though. I was able to have fun with them without feeling guilty after the heart-to-heart I had shared with Andrew. I felt like I could really be myself, which was something I hadn't been able to do in a really long time. Collin criticized everything I said, and I had to put on some flawless act for him. There was no room for anything but his strict image of a girlfriend – which I had a really hard time following. I was too much of a "good girl" and I was too "uptight," but when I loosened up, I was a "slut" and "careless." I stood up for myself more than he liked, although I could have and should have stood up for myself a great deal more. I didn't like to party as much as he did. I was "too sensitive," but when I didn't let his words hurt me, I was "a total bitch." I was "obsessive and crazy," although he made me that way. Nothing was ever good enough for him.

I stayed with Amanda another night. I was safe there, and I couldn't risk letting myself fall for Collin again. We met up with her boyfriend and his friends at a bonfire. She was introducing me to everyone when he walked up. "Howdy, ma'am, I'm Austen," he greeted me as he grabbed my hand.

"I'm McKenzie," I forced myself to push out. I was hooked at that first hand shake. He was tall and tan with nice hair and boots. He sat with Amanda, Daniel, and I, as we talked by the fire.

"Are you cold?" he politely asked me as he noticed that I was shivering.

"Yeah, a little." He took off his jacket and put it around me, brushing my neck with his hand as he pulled his arms back to his side. Austen was something new and exciting, and I finally saw myself with someone other than Collin. The night was nearing dawn and the fire was decreasing.

"Y'all ready to go?" Daniel asked as he turned to Amanda and me.

"Yeah," I replied as I stood up. Austen walked us to Daniel's truck. "Here's your jacket." I started taking it off when he put his hand on my shoulder.

"Are you still cold?"

"Yeah," I told him.

"Keep it," he said as he smiled, "I'll get it another time." I smiled back at him as I got in and shut the door. I prayed that I would have to see him again to give his jacket back. It got me a guy once before. Not only did I want it to work again, I *needed* it to work again. I needed anything and everything to satisfy me before I would cave and go back to Collin.

It was obvious to everyone that I found Austen undeniably amazing. Amanda was probably more excited than I was, and arranged for us to all go eat dinner together the next night. I was nearing a panic attack as she calmed me down when Daniel texted Amanda that they were on their way to pick us up. I hadn't seriously considered ever actually being with someone else, and I suddenly forgot everything to do with a new guy. I didn't know what to say or how to act. I didn't know if I should play hard to get or be easy to get or just be myself, which was actually the most difficult thing for me to be. I didn't know what *myself* was anymore. I didn't want to be too hard to get, because I didn't want to chance him thinking I wasn't interested, which I was, and I didn't want to be easy for him to get because Collin taught me that easy is boring, and that was the last thing I wanted to be. It was tough to balance it all. It was a delicate situation, and I couldn't mess up. Austen was the only guy who made me excited to move on. I went to dinner with terrible nervous jitters, but I assumed that I did well because we completely hit it off.

Austen impacted my life much more than he will ever know. He was so much to me. He was my hope, my freedom. I saw in him a new life for myself. I was finally ready to let go of Collin and everything he had done to me. Collin always told me that I would never find another guy. No other guy could ever love me. There's nothing to love about me, really. I was boring and dramatic all at the same time, I gave him a hard time way too often and I didn't deserve him. He loved me despite my many flaws, and it scared him. He didn't want to be with me so he pushed me away by cheating on me. I believed all of it for a long while. Austen made me second-guess all of it. He complimented me and always had his arms around me. He seemed genuinely happy when we were together, and I actually felt happy for the first time in a long time. Austen gave me my confidence back for a little while, and I held on so tight. I wouldn't, couldn't let go of it. We shared hot chocolate fireside kisses and deep conversation until he would pull me up to dance. I would catch myself laughing and realize that for a moment I had completely forgotten about Collin. Nothing would have made me let go of that feeling.

The four of us were inseparable until my 16th birthday a few weeks later. I had just begun settling into the fact that I might be done with Collin, and I found myself opening up to Austen. The four of us, along with a few other friends of mine through Amanda, went to a cabin at the lake for the weekend. It was November, which meant alcohol and cuddling around a fire. It was great, until I had a little too much to drink. The last thing I remember was walking across a bridge with Austen until I woke up alone and completely naked the next morning. I walked outside still partially drunk and found Austen talking to the guys and drinking a beer. I put my arms around him and he put his arm around me as he kissed me on the forehead. I smiled and went to pack my things. We left the lake and Austen dropped me off at my mom's house. He hugged me bye, and I never heard from him again. A few days went by of texting him with no response. Amanda was acting strange and Austen was ignoring me, and I became absolutely devastated. Everything I had gained I lost in one drunken night.

I sat alone in my room starting back at square one, and once again was waiting for a period that didn't come on time. I had no friends and no plans and was terrified that something was growing in me once again, and I did my best to not break down. I had walked to Brent's house with him and his friend, Brandon, after school one day. My jeans were tight and I was feeling sick to my stomach. Brent didn't know about my potential second pregnancy, and I was reluctant to tell him. Eventually I had to, asking for some of his shorts to change into. I thought he would be disappointed in me, or even drop me like everyone else had. Instead, he was supportive and made it a game. He put on my shirt and some bikini bottoms he found, Brandon put on my jeans, and I put on Brandon's sweatshirt and Brent's shorts. We took funny, cross-dressed pictures and he made me forget all of my worries and made me laugh again. Brent couldn't truly make me feel better, though. I needed someone there for me. If I was going to have a baby, I needed a guy to care for us. Brent had no intention of being that guy. I texted Austen enough times with no response to take the hint – he wanted nothing to do with me, even if I was carrying his child. I waited as long as I possibly could, but I eventually caved and messaged Collin on Facebook. He instantly responded. He was always there for me when no one else was. That's how he pulled me in time and time again. Once again, I clung to the only thing that would let me. I could actually drive now, so I met him at the park. I got out of my car and into his truck. I sat as far away from him as possible when I first got in, telling him every detail of Austen. Eventually he held out his arms and I sunk into them. I cried as I told him I could be pregnant. He told me that he would support me and a child, which I should have known was a complete lie considering what he had done when I actually was pregnant, but it was exactly what I wanted to hear. I wanted to believe him so badly that I blocked out reality. He held my face and kissed me sweetly. "I love you, McKenzie, and I will be good to you. I'm sorry for the things I've said before, and I'm going to make it up to you." I held onto that for weeks, replaying it over and over again in my mind.

Collin and I didn't see each other much for the next few weeks and didn't define our relationship. I knew he would be cheating on me anyway, so there was no point to put a label on us. I wanted to be able to leave him as easily as I possibly could, and in order to do that, I needed to distance myself from him as much as possible. It's like I had to wean myself off of him. I couldn't take a clean break from him. I needed him too badly. It made it easier that I had been having a lot more success in school my sophomore year. The people who made my life miserable had all graduated, and I rarely saw any of my old friends. I wasn't involved in any activities and I kept myself as invisible as I possibly could. I kept my personal life completely secret to the people I did talk to, who were all random people in my classes.

In my art class, I sat at a table with another girl in my grade, Diana. We made small talk more and more every day, and eventually became friends. She invited me to go with her to her boyfriend's basketball game one night, and I agreed to go. I didn't have to ask Collin or even tell him. For all I knew, he was with another girl anyway, and at this point, I didn't even care. All I wanted was to do something with myself that I was in control of.

I picked Diana up that night and brought us to the basketball game at her boyfriend's school which was about thirty minutes away and in another division for sports than our school. I knew absolutely nobody except Diana, and that was the best feeling that I had had in months. There was no pressure for me to act a certain way or to be concerned with what everyone was thinking about me. Collin didn't know where I was and I could talk to whoever I wanted to without worrying about someone watching me and telling Collin. Nobody was paying any attention to me, and I loved it. There were no whispers and giggles coming from behind me, there were no mean stares from people I passed. I got to relax for once in a really long time.

After the game was over, I met Josh, Diana's boyfriend, and Joey, his best friend. They invited us to go to Joey's house, and we said yes. I brought Diana to pick up some extra clothes and we headed to Joey's, which was just down the road from my house, but right over the district line. They pulled out the water bong, and I watched for a while as they got high. I had seen Collin smoke and even roll his own blunts, but I had never tried it. I eventually took a hit, and couldn't stop coughing. One hit was enough for me for the night. I didn't think smoking would be a habit I would pick up. We ended up going to Waffle House late at night, and when we arrived back, Diana and Josh went to the guest bedroom. I texted my mom telling her that I was staying at Diana's for the night so I could stay out longer with my new friends. I didn't want to leave. My chances of giving in and messaging Collin were way higher with me alone than me with friends. Besides, Joey was the perfect combination of good and bad. He was a sort of bad boy, but was a good person. He had morals but knew how to have fun. That's exactly what I was expecting and hoping to find in Collin. Joey and I stayed up talking all night until he told me I could sleep in his bed and he would sleep on the couch. Through talking that night, I found out that Joey was undeniably perfect, and he found out that I had lost myself to a guy that never really loved me. It's unfortunate that it took me seeing several perfect guys for me and screwing things up with them to finally realize that Collin wasn't good enough for me. Joey was one of those guys. We both liked each other, and he took things really slow with me because he knew what I had been through.

Joey started out being plenty enough to distract me from Collin. Joey didn't know who the guy was in my life that helped me burn it all to ash, and I didn't know that Joey and Collin were friends. I hadn't even talked to Collin in a couple of weeks. I had been spending all of my time at Joey's apartment with Josh and Diana, especially since Christmas Break was upon us and I had nothing better to do than to party it up with my new friends. Joey was having a party at his house, and the four of us started early. I had tried smoking again. I didn't like it any more the second time around, but I needed something to make me as high as he did. I couldn't imagine us having a normal relationship anymore, but I didn't think I could ever feel as intensely as he made me feel ever again. I searched for passion in all the wrong places, and always came out lacking. All I could feel was numbness, so I pushed myself, closer and closer to rock bottom, hoping I could make myself feel something. I made myself laugh louder and constantly kept myself busy with high hopes that I could convince even myself that I could find whatever it was that I was looking for. I was high and dancing around with Joey when Collin walked in the door. Both of our jaws dropped. I was too high to come up with a solution. I just stood there with my arms around Joey. Collin looked shocked. All I could do was laugh as Chase was trying to pull him out of Joey's house. Collin pulled away from him and walked up to me.

"What the hell are you doing?" he asked me.

"Dancing" was all I could come up with. He went back and talked to Chase for a few minutes. Chase came all the way in and shut the door. They both ignored me, and I kept dancing on Joey. It was easy, until we all sat in a circle and took turns taking hits on the water bong. I sat next to Joey, and Collin sat next to me. Thankfully the weed took the edge off, and even made the awkward and possibly dangerous situation kind of funny.

The next morning, I told Joey that Collin was the one that I had told him about that first night we had stayed up talking. Joey and I had been doing well together. We weren't anything serious or official, but we liked each other and had a lot of fun together. The short amount of time we were friends was enough to make me want to leave Collin. My friendship with Joey made me believe that more guys than I previously thought didn't want to just use me like Austen did. I thought there could be a better boyfriend out there, but I wasn't sure I was good enough to have any better than Collin. Joey had people over almost every night while his mom was at work. Collin started to become one of those people. I focused on Joey, and it drove Collin insane. He was incredibly mad and upset all in one, but tried to be really nice to me at the same time. He seemed uneasy at the fact that I had a life outside of him, and more importantly, a guy other than him. I finally had control over him, and I loved it. What I had with Joey became part of a game to make Collin jealous. I wanted to torment him as long as he would let me.

The more I saw Collin, the more difficult it was to stay away from him. I had a crush on Joey since I had met him, and my feelings for him had been genuine at one point, but they were miniscule compared to what I felt for Collin. It was impossible to emotionally get over him when he was constantly around. Making him want me became my sole focus. The feelings I did have for Joey faded as Collin started to show me that he wanted me. While in the arms of Joey, I would be making sure that Collin was watching. He would give me that smile that I couldn't resist. Me and Collin slipped into flirting that eventually progressed into subtle long hugs bye and playful touching as we passed each other. Everything I worked to move past crumbled around me. I knew what I was letting myself go back to, but I couldn't find the power in me to stop. The temptation overcame me, and in one drunken night we went right back to where we left off. Deep down I hated myself for slipping back into his grasp, but I thought that I had it under control. I thought that I finally knew how to keep him satisfied enough to only be with me, and I thought that I had just over exaggerated his violent outbursts. Thinking that I had control being with him, though, cost me the biggest loss of control I had suffered yet.

I kept thinking Collin would change for me despite how many times he had proven me wrong. The more he cheated on me, the closer I got to being done with him. By Christmas break almost exactly one year after we met, I had conformed to what I thought he wanted me to be. I stopped caring about everything like I had in the past. Despite my best efforts, though, I couldn't keep him away from other girls. I occasionally got texts from people telling me that he had been with other girls at parties he went to. Sometimes I would bring it up, but I knew there was no point. I went to a party at Joey's house while he went to a different party with some of his friends. I got a text from a girl telling me that she wasn't sure if me and Collin were still together, but she thought that I should know he had gone into a bedroom with a girl. I called him until he answered. I could tell he was high, and I could hear a girl asking who was on the phone in the background. I hung up the phone, took shots with Diana, and called Trevor, a guy in a few of my classes at school.

Trevor came to Joey's, and I did what I did best at the time – I had fun. By this time, I knew that Collin was bad for me. I knew that he drew on a dark place inside of me that only came out when he was on my mind. I had slipped into a cycle, though, and I was utterly addicted. In the past, I was so logical and responsible. I did what I was supposed to do when I was supposed to do it. I anxiously weighed decisions before I made them. Somewhere through the long heartbreak that Collin had caused me, I stopped caring about everything except having fun. Trevor was good for me for a while, but I got bored quickly. I didn't want a boyfriend, I just wanted to have a good time. We were good while we lasted, and that was longer than I expected. I caught a glimpse of what a relationship should look like. He respected me. While we were together, I was the only girl he talked to. There was no girl on the side when I wasn't around. He took things slow and never pushed me to do anything I was uncomfortable with. He made me laugh, and we never fought. I tried to make myself have feelings for Trevor, but I couldn't. He kept me away from Collin for a little while, however, the craving never went away. I couldn't tell anyone my feelings, especially him, so I wrote them down with no intention of acting on them.

"I haven't cried for you in a while, but tonight I did. For the past couple of days, I've been longing for you in a way that I haven't before. The only trace of you left in my life is the shirt of yours that I'm wearing as I write this. Memories of us are sprinkled around me everywhere I go, though, somehow making your presence linger. You took a wrecking ball to my life without hesitation and with no intention of ever looking back. Everything is changing. I met a guy, and while he is absolutely perfect, he isn't you. He knows what to say and do to be everything I should want. There's something missing, though. I want you back, so desperately, and after everything you've done to me, I have no idea why. You built me up so high, and then you crushed me. You were everything to me, and I would have done anything to make you happy for the rest of my life. I already gave up so much for you. I was always yours, from the moment I met you. You were and always would have been enough for me. I have pretended to be happy with high hopes that I could eventually fool myself into believing it, but so far it has been unsuccessful. My mom always told me that the guy I'm with should make it known that I'm his absolute favorite person, that he should do absolutely anything to prove his love for me. I haven't always believed that I was worth some grand gesture as she claims, but after much thought, I agree with her. I just hoped that you would become that guy for me. I always thought that my love for you would overcome all of the challenges we would face. I have known for some time that you have personal issues that run deeper than you let anyone see. I thought I had gotten in, broken down your wall you built up. Maybe I did, and maybe that's why you pushed me away. Everyone tells me that I should hate you. Part of me agrees, but deep down I feel like you're just misunderstood. I have been holding on to all of the promises you made, praying that you would somehow find it in your heart to keep those promises and come back to me. I have lost so much for you, and I would do it all over again if it meant I could have you. Nobody understands it, including myself, but love has never been rational."

I was feeling really vulnerable. I had to get away for a few days. I couldn't risk losing Trevor and the respect of all my friends and family again for going back to Collin. I didn't see my cousin Bailey often, but I packed a bag and drove to her house two hours away. She didn't ask me about Collin, and I didn't want to tell her. She was one of the only people left in my life that didn't know about all of the stupid decisions I had made. We met up with a few of her friends that night and I tried to have fun. We had all been drinking for a while when one of the guys wanted to give me a tour of the house. I followed him into his room. He sat on the bed and asked me to sit down next to him. We talked for a few minutes until he tried to kiss me, unbuttoning my pants. I pushed him off of me and Bailey opened the door. I quickly got up and ran out, not saying a word the entire ride back to her house. I felt violated, and all I wanted was to call Collin.

I woke up the next morning feeling really sad. I didn't know who I was anymore. I had become some person devoted to getting Collin to feel something – jealousy, anger, love, passion, anything. I lost myself in the process. I had always been the good girl, and I wanted to get that back, I just didn't know how. I cut my trip short and headed back home. I went to Joey's house with Diana. I didn't tell Trevor that I was back in town yet. I wanted a little more time away from him. The three of us were smoking as I was eating cereal straight out of the box. Collin walked through the door, looked at me laughing and asked if I was high. I looked at Diana and she poured me a shot. One shot turned into three, and Collin started rubbing his hands on me. I called Trevor and told him to come get me. I couldn't resist Collin, and I knew that the best thing for me to do was leave. Trevor was already drunk by the time he got to Joey's. We went back to his house and drank more. Wanting to be with someone that I couldn't be with was painful, and I was self-medicating with liquor and Trevor.

The next thing I remember is laying in Joey's bed. I heard him and Diana yelling about Trevor. The cup that I thought was filled with water had actually been tequila. Joey came into his room to check on me. All I could tell him was to make the room stop spinning. I got out of the bed and tried my hardest to find my way to the toilet. I tripped and flipped over the couch and ran into the wall face first before making it out of the door of his room. I threw up in the sink and all over the floor. Diana cleaned me off while Joey cleaned his bathroom. I woke up the next morning with lots of shame and the intention of never drinking again. I apologized to Joey and Diana hundreds of times. They assured me that they weren't mad at me, but I was still embarrassed I let myself get as bad as I did

Diana was still mad at Trevor for not taking better care of me, but she tolerated him. He joined us at Joey's house for a movie. Collin and Chase came in unannounced and not invited. Collin looked surprised when he saw Trevor's arm around me, and Trevor looked scared. He took his arm off of me. Collin broke the silence, "as long as you don't touch her, we will be fine." I looked at him and laughed sarcastically, scooting closer to Trevor. Things got very heated very quickly as me and Collin were screaming at each other. Trevor sat quietly, Chase and Joey were pulling Collin out of the room, and Diana was trying to get me to calm down. They got Collin into the living room, and I sat down to continue watching my movie. It didn't affect me – I had seen much worse from Collin before. Trevor walked into the living room and came back into the bedroom frantically telling me that we needed to leave. He argued with me, telling me that it didn't matter that we had gotten there first. I sighed loudly as a display of my annoyance as I grabbed my purse. I walked into the living room to see Joey and Chase holding Collin back. With clenched fists, he yelled at me telling me he was going to fight Trevor. Before I could even roll my eyes, Trevor had ran down the stairs and to his car. I crossed my arms and said "you're pathetic" as I walked out.

Trevor left before I could even make it to my car. I couldn't understand why he got so scared. Deep down, I was terrified of Collin, but Trevor was much bigger and stronger than me. The fact that someone more capable of self-defense than I was ran as quickly as he did made me even more scared of Collin. I needed someone that I knew I could count on to protect me and stand up to him if needed. I didn't want to admit it, but seeing Collin get so jealous lit a spark in me again. I stayed strong, though, and kept my distance from Collin even after I stopped talking to Trevor.

I had felt lost for a while, and I knew the best way to find myself was to focus solely on me, leaving no room for boys in my life. I made an effort to surround myself with positivity – repairing my relationship with my mom, spending time with friends I could trust, and being as adventurous as I possibly could. For the first time in a long time, I stopped looking for the next guy to get my mind off of Collin. I stayed as busy as possible to keep my mind on anything but Collin. I submerged myself in my schoolwork, I started talking to my mom more when she got home from work, and I tried to have fun with my friends.

I went on a weekend trip to the lake that consisted of fires and mudding with Diana, Joey, and a few other people. I was actually having fun, and for a little while, Collin didn't cross my mind at all. Because of that weekend, I felt some hope of the future. I felt like maybe I could be done with him and just learn to have fun. After everything he did to me, I knew that I shouldn't even want to be with him. I finally began to see what my family and friends saw from the beginning. He was a snag in my perfect high school path, and while it would always be a part of my past, I could get back on track and have the life I was supposed to. Girls like me didn't get wrapped up in guys like him – they were with the good guys, like Brent. I promised myself that I would be single until I was ready, and then I would try again with Brent.

With Collin seemingly out of my life permanently, I began to have a real social life again. My main focus would be having fun rather than trying to forget Collin, trying to make him jealous, or looking for ways to replace him in my life. He was like a drug to me, and I thought I was finally clean. My post-Collin addicted life was bright and colorful. I worked on mending broken relationships with friends and family and found myself laughing louder and smiling bigger than I had in the past year. I had friends to talk to during the week and parties to go to on the weekends. I was finally doing the things that I imagined I would do during high school. I finally had in my grasp what I had been longing for. I still felt like something was missing from my life, though, and I relied on Brent to fill that gap.

I did my best to take things slow with Brent, working on being friends again first. I knew that it would be my last chance to make any kind of relationship work with him. I was excited to have my nightly phone calls with Brent again. I forgot what they felt like for a while. We met up soon after we started talking again. I felt like I could be myself with him, but I wasn't quite sure of who I was without Collin. He became part of my identity. I had liked Brent for so long, and I wanted more than anything to forget about Collin and have my fairytale life with Brent.

It had been a while since Collin stayed on my mind constantly. What he was doing crossed my mind occasionally, but the thought never stayed for long and it was getting less by the day. On my way home from Brent's house one night, I saw Collin's truck. Without thought, I followed him. Eventually he pulled up to a house that I had never seen before. Jealousy overcame me. I wanted to know who he was meeting so badly that I seriously considered getting out of my car and looking in the window in an attempt to figure out who he was going to see. I came to my senses and went home, telling myself to calm down and focus on how good my life was without him. It didn't take away my jealousy, though. I couldn't stand the thought of him with another girl. It made me so sick that I didn't sleep that entire night.

For the next couple of weeks, I would drive past Chase's house to see if Collin's truck was there. It wasn't far from my house, so I would just make an extra turn on the way home from school or to Brent's house. Sometimes his truck was there, sometimes it wasn't. When it was, I would question who all was there and what he was doing. At first when his truck wasn't there, I would worry about where he was. After a little while, I began actively trying to find him. I would go all over town from Collin's house to Jeremy's house and even to Amanda's house when I felt really desperate. When I couldn't find it after all that, I began to get mad. I was used to him fighting to get me back after we broke up. I took comfort in the fact that he wanted me. It drove me insane to know that he was living a new life without me.

Despite the new and constant obsession running through my mind, I continued with my life as normally as I possibly could. I kept up conversations with Brent and spent even more time with Diana in an attempt to get my mind off Collin again. Brent had lost me before because he moved too slowly. This time, though, I wanted us to move slowly. I counted on it – I was forcing myself to try to be with him so I wouldn't go back to Collin. I still couldn't even grasp the idea of actually being with someone else. I was in a fragile state and needed to be handled delicately. He was different than he had been before, more assertive, more direct. While that may have kept me before, it scared me off. The more he pushed me into a relationship, the more I pulled away. I wasn't anywhere near ready to be with him and I shouldn't have started talking to him again as quickly as I did. I knew that Brent was a good guy, but he didn't make me feel anything. Collin constantly gave me a rush of emotions that no one else seemed to be able to give me. Following him gave me a hint of emotions again. Although the feelings were negative, at least I was feeling something. I tried to talk myself into staying with Brent, slowing down a bit and putting some focus back on rediscovering myself. I thought that if I could find something healthy and productive to be passionate about in place of Collin, I could be content with myself and then have a successful relationship with Brent.

It seemed as if Collin could sense when I was feeling vulnerable. I longed for him, but I had a plan and a lot of hope. I was going to be done with him. I wanted to be clean and sober, moving on from my addiction to him and throwing myself into something good. I was going to allow my bad decisions to make me a better person, working that much harder to make a difference in the world. I wanted to completely forgive my mom and do something that she would actually be proud of. When Collin started messaging me on Facebook, though, all of those plans went on hold. At first, I would ignore the messages. I had too much going for me to throw it all away on him again. I held my ground. Eventually, though, I started to feel bad for him. He went from trying to just start a conversation to telling me he missed me and wanted me back. He said that he knew he messed up, he just needed one more chance with me but he knew that he didn't deserve it. It made me feel good to hear that, but at the same time, I wondered if one last chance was all he really needed to make a change. It was the longest we had ever been broken up, and I thought that maybe he learned his lesson. I pushed that to the back of my mind, though, and politely told him that it was best that we go our separate ways. He told me that he was at the end of my street and I needed to go see him for a few minutes to make sure that staying apart was what I really wanted. I knew my mom would be home soon, and if I didn't go, he would sit there in his truck and argue with me. I went quickly to prevent my mom from seeing him. We drove around my block and talked about everything that had happened in the last year. He made me feel like I was making a mistake, that the kind of love we had was a once in a lifetime kind of experience. I knew he was right, and I found it difficult to resist him. No other guy had ever given me even a fraction of the feelings that Collin did. Even with all of the bad, I reveled in the passion of our relationship. I told him that I would think about what we talked about, and that was enough to satisfy him. He dropped me off at the end of my street and I walked home in tears.

Against my better judgement, I decided that I wanted to give Collin another chance without actually being invested in the relationship. I wanted to get close to him without actually putting a label on us. I thought that if I could be with him with no emotional ties, I could protect myself from getting hurt. All I knew was that I would never find what we had anywhere else. Me and Collin had a magnetic attraction. I lived for the highs he gave me and the sweet promises that he made. I didn't believe real love existed anymore. There was no point to start over with someone else. I didn't want to get my hopes up, believing that there was more to love just to get my heart broken again. I knew what to expect with Collin, and I thought that there was no way we could get worse. I talked to Brent and my friends by day and saw Collin by night. I made a web of lies, telling everyone stories so they wouldn't find out I was even associating myself with Collin again.

My communication with the outside world withered away as my nightly visits with Collin grew longer. I eventually stopped talking to Brent altogether and only talked to my friends at school. I started to let my guard down with him again, getting too comfortable in the beginning stage of our getting back together. We rarely argued, we laughed a lot, and we had the most fun right after getting back together, pulling me in deep once again. I wanted this time with him to be the last time with him. I thought it was different. I thought that through the time that we had been apart, we both changed a little bit. I had new confidence and I thought he was going to treat me right. He altered my state of mind in a way that nothing else could. Before I knew it, he tore me apart bit by bit all over again. I thought that I was strong enough to not let him hurt me, but all of the confidence that I had gained while we were apart was quickly shattered as he degraded everything about me. He couldn't stand the fact that I had talked to Brent while we were broken up. He told me it was slutty, and questioned if I was over Brent. He told me that my boobs were too small and my legs were too big. He swore that my vagina had gotten looser since the last time we broke up. Everything I started to feel good about crashed and burned. With all of that wrong with me, I didn't think another guy would ever want to be with me. When he loved on me, though, it was like I won some unattainable treasure. He built me up almost as quickly as he tore me down, and I relied on his perception of me to feel good about myself. I tried to fit the mold I thought he wanted, and I didn't even know who I was when I came out of it all. All I knew was that I was desperate for Collin to love me. He was holding us together, and the longer I was with him, the more of myself I lost.

9

DEATH

I laid under clothes and broken shelves in the closet, hiding from him and hoping that he had forgotten where he had left me. I felt like I had been there for days, but I assumed it had just been a few hours. My head was hurting too badly to judge how much time had passed. My heart hurt worse than my head did, though, and my eyes were raw from the tears I had cried until I couldn't cry any more. I watched blood from my nose drip onto the white carpet. Before I met Collin, that would have been something that I would have actually cared about. Stains were the least of my problems, though. I just stared at it, worrying about what was to come when Collin came back. I curled myself into a ball and held my ripped shirt over my back, picturing the rage flaring in his eyes and trying to pinpoint the exact moment that caused what happened that night.

My patience had been growing thinner and thinner after every incident. I hoped for just nights without fighting. Sometimes my hopes were granted, but I knew that a relationship was supposed to be something more. I knew that our best wasn't good enough. Even at my lowest, I knew I deserved happiness. Collin didn't make me happy anymore. My happiest days at this point were those that I wasn't scared of him. The easy solution would be to just break up with him and move on with my life. It was a fragile situation, though. I was genuinely scared of what would happen if I ended things. He was cruel even when I tried my hardest. My happiness wasn't my top priority – my safety was. I wasn't sure what a life without him would look like. My old life had slipped away long ago and there was no returning. I wasn't sure I wanted my old life anymore, anyway. I believed that I had nothing and nobody but him. I would be starting over from a point that made me feel vulnerable. There was a small part of me that still desperately wanted me and Collin to work. He promised me everything I hoped for out of life. No matter how small, that tiny part of me kept me holding on. It was a constant, internal battle.

Collin had been happy that night. I felt safe.

"I don't think I can do this anymore," I told him hesitantly, not sure what I really wanted to come from that statement.

He looked at me with the sweetest smile, asking "what do you mean?"

"You know what I mean, Collin."

He reached his arm over me and kissed me on the forehead. I was relieved – I got through that talk alive, and even better than I had hoped for.

"McKenzie," he said apologetically, "I am sorry for everything I've put you through. I will never hurt you again, I promise. I'm yours." He nestled his head in my hair and I tried to relax. I wanted to believe him so badly.

I kept watching the movie we had on and he kept texting who I had hoped was just a friend. He got up to get something out of the kitchen and I saw his phone light up. I glanced at it and saw that it was a girl he had been texting. That's when it hit me – I was done – for real this time. He was taking a while in the kitchen, so I ran to the closet in Joey's room. I unlocked his phone with a password I wasn't supposed to know. It wasn't just one girl that he was talking to, but several. He was asking one for naked pictures, making plans to hang out with another, and talking about me to the third. He told her that he wanted to be with her instead of me. I didn't want to know what I would've seen with a little more time.

The closet door opened, and he was almost as furious as I was. I took too long. He noticed that I took his phone. I felt hot as he screamed at me to not go through his phone. I wanted to scream back, but I couldn't find my voice. I was speechless. Anger overwhelmed me and I knew that I stood no chance against him, but I tried to slap him in the face anyway. He grabbed my arm and slung me into the wall. I pushed him as hard as I could in an attempt to get him away from the closet door so I could escape. He pushed me back and I successfully punched him in the face. He grabbed my head and slammed me into the wall. I felt a little dizzy and black filled my eyes as I fell to the ground. I tried to get up on my own, but he picked me up by my neck. He dropped me to the ground as Courtney pulled him away from me. His focus switched from me to her, and I ran. I couldn't find my keys in the few seconds I had before Collin's focus switched back to where I had gone. I ran frantically to the kitchen when I heard him coming. I got in the pantry, hoping that he wouldn't find me. He opened the door and Courtney tried to pull him away. He elbowed her in the face, causing her to stumble back.

We heard a loud knock on the door and all froze. Courtney opened the door to two police officers. They asked if we were all just getting high together. She lied and told the cops that it was just Collin. She put her arms around me as she told them how he choked me and pushed me into the wall, and how he elbowed her in the face. I felt so low at that point. I was embarrassed to be one of those girls in domestic disputes. I told them that I didn't want to press charges when they asked, and I instantly regretted it. I was afraid, though. I had tried to press charges before, and it only made things worse. I didn't trust the police system. I knew that I missed my chance to get him taken away, though. I missed my chance to find a way out. The cops brought Collin outside to search his truck. I prayed that they would find something. They came back upstairs a few minutes later without Collin. They made him go home, buying me some time to collect my thoughts.

I went back to the closet where it all started and looked in the mirror. My shirt was ripped. I wanted to be upset about the shirt, but I wasn't. It was one of my favorite shirts, but all I could think about was how I wouldn't be going anywhere anytime soon. I had big red marks on my arms where he hands squeezed me. I knew that it was just a matter of time before they turned blue. Something had scratched my leg in the kitchen. I didn't feel it at the time, but it started throbbing as soon as I noticed it was there. My face was what troubled me the most, though. I looked unhealthy. I had bags under my eyes and I had lost the color in my cheeks. I had lost all of my energy. I laid down in the closet as I contemplated death. He could have killed me if he really wanted to. Part of me wished that he did. A small piece of me always told me to keep pushing. That hope is what kept me with Collin, and I hated it, but in the end it was what showed me that there was light at the end of the tunnel. Hope always overpowered all of my other emotions.

I felt scared as I laid in the closet. I didn't know who I could trust. I didn't even trust myself. It was at that moment that I realized a part of me had died. Every day I asked myself who I was supposed to be, and I knew I didn't want to have to ask myself that anymore. I squeezed my eyes shut tightly and prayed – something I hadn't done in a while. I thanked God for keeping me alive. I didn't know what to ask him for. I had no idea where my life was supposed to be headed – I just asked for him to do *something*. I wasn't even sure what I wanted anymore. My life needed a change, though. I eventually dozed off and woke up to hear the closet door open.

"Collin?" Silence filled the air while he looked me up and down.

"No, he's gone. You're safe now." Joey had come to my rescue once again. He calmed me down. He made me sane, able to sort through my scattered thoughts.

For a few months, I had known that something had to change. My body was breaking. My mind was worse. I was beginning to lose any sense of concentration. I was too aware of every word and action of myself. I had been upsetting Collin more and more, and I was terrified of what he would do to punish me next. Joey held me tightly in his bed, trying to calm me down. I didn't get much sleep. I was terrified that Collin would come back. Joey made me feel safe, but I knew that Collin would win in a fight. He would kill both of us if he saw us lying together, but I stayed anyway. I spent the night searching my memories of where it went wrong. I guess it always was wrong, from the beginning. I just didn't see it. What I saw was a lie. I lost myself, or rather, he took myself from me. He gave me nothing to cling to but him. He deceived me into thinking that I couldn't even trust myself. He twisted reality; he twisted my thoughts. I was to blame – for everything. I made him feel insecure - he cheated on me. I was out of line – he pushed me around. I had drowned in his lies and his deceit long ago. His charm grabbed me and pulled me in, with no intention of ever letting go. He had sucked the life out of me. That was his entertainment. He thrived on my pain. He smirked as I cried and begged him to love me. He was the only voice I had heard for months, but I gained strength as his lies crumbled around me.

My mind was constantly filled with distorted thoughts, swirling around relentlessly – something I only realized after I was away from him. I didn't know I had a choice to leave. He didn't let me dream of another life. He knew the consequences of that. If he let me think that I could leave, I would. I looked back at all of the good and noticed that the good only happened after the bad; after I was hanging on by a thread. He had to weave me in deeper – just deep enough to where I would give him one more chance to take more from me. I found my keys and left when it was still dark. I drove to my mom's house, going 20 minutes out of my way taking back-roads, hoping that nobody, especially Collin, would find me. He would punish me if he found me. If he somehow found me, he would find a way to stop me from getting inside my house. He would find his way into my car, drag me out, and hurt me worse than he ever had before. I closed the garage quickly so that he couldn't know if I was there or not. I pictured all of the threats he had made in the past and cringed, knowing that there was a really good chance that he would actually do all of those things to me if he knew I was there. Insane anger overcame my body. I hated him. When I pictured high school, I never imagined that I would experience what I did. I had no idea how someone could take something so pure and happy and rip it open and crush it until it was nothing. That's what I was; nothing. I was nothing but a broken little girl with so much hope. I hoped for a lot of things. I hoped that I could make Collin happy and I hoped that he would have the best life possible. I did my very best to do that for him. I received the opposite in return. I felt foolish as I sneakily unlocked the door and instantly locked it behind me after I got inside. Nobody should be as scared as I was to be seen. I crawled into bed and instantly fell asleep.

The next morning was different than every morning for the past year. I woke up hating Collin, not craving him. I woke up from my sad state as Collin's toy. I blared Taylor Swift songs all day, probably taking "Picture to Burn," a little too literally as I gathered all of the pictures I had printed out of us over the past year. It wasn't enough, though. I took all of Collin's stuff that he had left at my house and threw it all in the fireplace with the pictures, watching it burn until it was all ash. I gathered all of it in a bag and walked outside. With the cold January breeze blowing, I dumped the bag upside down and watched as the remnants of our memories blew away. I took a deep breath in, and told myself that I would never settle for anything less than I deserve ever again. I wanted nothing of him anywhere near me or in my sight. The handprints Collin made around my neck and arms would be the last thing Collin ever left me with. They would fade quicker than the pain he had caused me, but with time, it would all disappear and I would be okay in the end. I finally had enough.

A few weeks later, he messaged me, begging me to give him another chance. He was always so good with hand-picking each word and carefully stringing them together, and I knew that this wasn't any different. I knew deep down that it was an empty promise, just like every other promise he had ever made. I wasn't ready to admit it before this, though. I wasn't ready to show the world that I was wrong and they were all right. I fell for him over and over again. He drew me in closer to him every time I thought about leaving him. Hope always was stronger than any other feeling for me. I had such strong hope that he would change for me. I wanted to marry him. I didn't know who I was without him. I couldn't bear the thought of another guy ever touching me. Every single touch, every laugh, every kiss I shared with Collin was so precious to me. It made me feel alive. Nothing has ever compared to the moments that he made me feel good enough for him.

I never understood why he cheated on me as many times as he did. I thought it was my fault for a while. The blame always somehow was placed on me. I did everything I could to be better than those other girls. I went to a tanning booth every day and exercised as much as I could. All I ate was fruit for a really long time, starving myself with hopes that the lack of fat on my body would help me gain Collin's love. I thought that if I looked better I could actually compete with the girls he cheated on me with. My work was for nothing, and some part of me knew that it was a waste of time all along. Nothing I could ever do would have made him faithful to me, no matter how much I strived for perfection. I sat down and wrote another letter to add to my collection of letters I had written him over the past year. This one was to myself, though, to read in the future when the time was right.

> "Dear older version of me,
> You went through a really tough breakup in the past. When you were writing this, you didn't understand what you did to make him do the things he did. You felt like the past year was a bad dream that you couldn't wake up from. You wanted him to come back and pretend like nothing happened, but at the same time, you needed him to stay as far away from you as possible. The days have been emotional roller coasters where you have gone from feeling like this breakup was the absolute best thing that could

happen to you crying and just wanting him to hold you. It has been a confusing, painful few weeks back here in 2010. Just in case you forgot, he was still cheating on you and you were still scared for your life a year after being together. Nothing had changed, and nothing ever will. The last time you saw him, you tearfully thanked God for saving your life because you knew that you may have not lived if it weren't for divine intervention. Right now you want closure, but I'm denying it because I know better – he will have a hold over me for some time and I can't risk losing myself to him again. As you read this later, you will understand. My world has fallen apart completely, and I pray that by the time this letter is read, life is a little less messy. I can't possibly know what the future holds, but he will never deserve another chance. I don't care what he has done for you now, but you have to stay strong, for the girl writing this, for the girl that cried in the shower so many times because she thought she was worthless, for the girl that thought she was incapable of being loved. Demand respect. Be selfish. For once actually let God lead you and stop trying to control every aspect of your life. Stay patient and know that there is more than this. Be picky. You deserve so much more than Collin would have ever given you. I'm writing this because I'm hurting from mistakes I keep making. I keep putting my trust in the wrong places. Whatever leads you to read this, remember to trust me now. You'll be a different person then. You'll be stronger and wiser. Know your worth and don't rush things – wait for the man God has designed for you. Don't take him back, ever. Love yourself!

– 16 year old you"

6 YEARS LATER

College graduation is quickly approaching, and now my biggest concern is maintaining a GPR high enough to get into the graduate school of my choice. I talk to my mom on the phone every day and have amazing friends that build me up. I'm in a sorority and live three and a half long hours from my home town with an amazing roommate and two dogs that have stolen my heart. My year with Collin seems like a distant dream. I never imagined myself where I am now, and now I can't imagine myself ever being involved in something so destructive.

My dad and I had become very close after Collin and I broke up. He was very involved in my life. The one thing Collin proved good for was bringing me back in touch with my dad. Everything that Collin did to me was worth him pushing me to get my dad back for the short time that I had with him. He died two years after I finally let him back into my life, and I couldn't thank Collin more for giving me that time with him. When Collin heard the news, he sent me a heartfelt message telling me how sorry he was that he died. He cared about me and my dad's relationship. He thought that it was important for me to have contact with him. Without him, I may have not had the chance to get to know my dad again.

Brent was my walking partner at our high school graduation, just like we promised our freshman year. We're still friends and we still talk occasionally. He moved two hours away from our home town, and one hour away from where I am now. I always told myself I should give a relationship with him another chance, but we have grown into very different people. Besides, no time would ever be enough to mend all of the bridges I burned with him. He will always hold a special place in my heart, though, and I know that I will always hold one in his too.

Something had changed in me the last time I left Collin. I knew that I was done with him. I swore to myself that there would be no more second chances, no more late night messaging. The last time I saw him would actually be the last. A boy named Taylor who had noticed me around school had a class with April, and she encouraged him to introduce himself to me. The next morning before school started, he introduced himself to me in the hallway. We walked up and down the hall until we had to go to class. We met again for lunch, and again after school. We spent every waking moment together, and I loved every second of it. He made me feel safe. The broken pieces of me were slowly put back together.

Collin's number was blocked from my phone. He messaged me on Facebook as he always did to get me back. It always took very little for me to agree to see him, but it was different this time. I told him that I met someone – Taylor, who was a year younger than Collin. Collin cussed at me and called me names, only proving to me how much I needed to stay away from him. He didn't stop messaging me, though. Taylor would politely respond, telling Collin that I was with him now and that I wasn't interested in rekindling my past relationship. I admired Taylor's patience with me. He knew I needed time to heal. He was honest and innocent, and he made me a better person. His undeniable respect for me made me respect myself more.

Despite my best effort to be done with Collin, he made even more of an effort to stay with me. He messed with my mind. It was always what he was best at. He threatened to kill me slowly, tying me upside down by my feet and stabbing me. He said I would bleed out as I watched him have sex with another girl. He said that he would chop me into pieces while I was still alive. He would mail the pieces to my mom, only keeping my boobs as a trophy on his wall. Collin went to the extent of messaging Taylor, telling him that he would fight him if he didn't leave me.

Taylor gave me hope for the future and helped me see a life beyond 17. The life I wanted wouldn't be possible if I stayed with Collin. I was terrified of him. I never slept through the night. I had nightmares of Collin taking me from my bedroom. He knew how to get into my house, and there was no doubt in my mind that he was crazy enough to do it. I was more scared of what Collin would do to me if I wasn't giving him what he wanted that what he would do to me if I stayed with him. He would have nothing to lose. If I went back to him, he wouldn't hurt me as badly. Taylor didn't give me that option. He didn't care what Collin said, he was going to protect me. He started staying at my house late enough to help me fall asleep. He eventually started staying late enough to comfort me when I woke up from nightmares. When I would wake up screaming, Taylor would already be holding me tightly. I would often push him off of me, half asleep, thinking that he was Collin. He would turn my lamp on and tell me that it was him, hugging me and kissing me on the forehead. He got me to fall back asleep and stay asleep, and finally the nightmares stopped altogether.

Despite how well my life seemed to be going, I still imagined how things could be with Collin if it weren't for the cheating, lying, and anger. I never admitted it, but I wanted him to change his ways and come back to me. I knew I didn't deserve what he did to me. I deserved better. I wanted him to be that person, though. It took me a while to start seeing my relationship with Taylor as something real. I had low expectations of a relationship after Collin. I was afraid that all guys would be like him. I loved Collin so much, and I was unsure that I would find any better. It was scary for me to go into a new relationship, not knowing what to expect. I had no way of knowing how things would be after a few months of being together. I trusted Collin in the beginning. I had no way of knowing if I was falling into another trap.

Something pushed me to give Taylor a fair chance. I knew he loved me deeper than Collin ever did. I could see it in his eyes when he looked at me. I was always his first priority, and I'll never forget that feeling. We reached a level of trust that I didn't know existed. I told him the most painful details of my life before he met me, and he took away my shame. He made me feel as if it wasn't all my fault, that I was not only a victim, but a survivor. He hated Collin for what he did to me, and he hated girls at our school for calling me names. He always stood up for me and assured me that Collin was to blame.

I had hoped that I would make a positive impact on Collin's life when I met him. In reality, though, his life went unchanged. I made no impact on his life while he tore mine apart. Everything he did had a sick twist. He manipulated me with every word, carefully stringed together. I realized that it was never actually him that I missed. I missed what he made me believe I had. I fell in love with a guy who had a "bad boy" front, but was soft and sweet on the inside. Despite knowing this, I had a hard time forgetting him. I wanted revenge, and I got it in my own way. While at the mall with Taylor a few months into our relationship, I saw Collin working in a shoe store. I made a huge effort to walk past holding Taylor's hand for Collin to see. That was the best revenge – making him watch me be happy with someone else.

One bright, sunny Friday morning I woke up to hear my phone ding. I had spent the whole night doing math homework and I was exhausted. I picked it up and saw an unusual message from a girl I didn't know. I was confused. I thought maybe it was some sort of spam at first. It read "I hope this doesn't sound crazy but I'm Collin's most recent ex and I was wondering if I could ask you a couple of questions. I'm just in a tough position and I need input from one of his ex's if it's not a big deal." After I gathered my thoughts and fully opened my eyes, I read the message over and over again with disappointment and fear – fear for her and fear for him. I heard that he was engaged, and I was happy for him. I was really hoping that this girl would be the one for him. I thought maybe he had changed in these few years and would finally be the man I always hoped he could be. She went on to tell me "My dad is pushing for me to press charges because he's been hurting me for a while ... I'm covered in over 40 cuts and bruises right now ... I feel terrible but he's almost killed me.." I hurt for this girl. I looked back at the situation and wondered if there was anything I could do differently. Maybe I could have pushed harder to get charges pressed. Maybe I could have sent him to jail and he wouldn't have hurt this girl. She asked me what Collin had done to me. I told her the truth. I think we both know what needed to be done. He needed to go to jail. Nobody deserves what Collin does. She had a detective come and take pictures, and swore to me that she would give me every detail of the process. I figured he'd go to jail in a couple of weeks. A month or so went by and I hadn't heard from her. As it turns out, she dropped the charges and got back with him. I can't say I don't blame her or that I don't understand. I got back with him a million times. I got back with him even after I had lost all hope of him changing. That's what Collin does to you. He makes you think that there is no other option. He makes you think that no other person will ever love you. With him, it's the only way to feel loved. You're not worth any more than he gives you, and you're not even worth that. He makes you feel like nothing, and he is the only one that can even begin to complete you. Somehow, though, he makes you love him, passionately and fully.

She has nobody left and nowhere to go – just like me in that same position four years ago. If nothing has changed, he's out cheating on her while she's at home crying with bruises he gave her before he left, although I hope that isn't the case. I messaged her, "Hey! I was just thinking about you! That probably sounds creepy but I hope you're doing okay. I don't really know you, but I do care. I felt very connected with you when you told me that you couldn't really talk to your friends because I know exactly how that feels. Every girl needs a girl to talk to. So I just wanted to let you know again that no matter what you have or haven't done or whatever is going on, you can always call or text me. I will always listen to you or offer advice if you ask for it. I won't judge you or make you feel stupid for anything you say. I'm sorry because I know this is probably weird, but like I said, I can always help you with anything. Or try at least." I gave her my number and she thanked me. She knows I understand her actions. I'm probably the only person that does, other than Amanda, maybe. She told me that they were trying to work things out, and that made me happy. She told me that despite what Collin had said, I was a good person and she was happy that we talked. Apparently she didn't hear very nice things about me. Nonetheless, I still wish him the best. He was just a guy that wanted to be loved, and had all the capability of being so. He was just scared. People say that love is the strongest feeling of all, but a lot of times, fear wins. It consumes us, little by little. He was drowned in the fear of getting hurt, and he pulled everyone he tried to love down with him. Shortly after our talk I saw a picture of the two of them, both dressed in black, with his friends and the caption "just married" under it.

I found that somehow in all of the stress of moving off to college away from everything I knew, I had fallen in love with my new life. Things were finally looking up for me. Taylor and I were together for almost four years until we finally ended our relationship on good terms. We grew apart. God sends people into our lives for certain periods of time to shape our lives in certain ways. Taylor is a very good man, but he is not the man that I am meant to spend the rest of my life with. He pulled me away from Collin and stood by my side through four very rough years. I can never thank him enough for holding me up through all the tears I cried and all the nights I couldn't sleep. We still love each other and care about each other, but we are two different people now, and he will always be my favorite person until I finally do meet Mr. Right.

I'm not afraid anymore, and I now have time to breathe. I am genuinely happy, and I don't have to question my safety. The nightmares of

Collin killing me had stopped and my paranoia of him finding me had ended. He planted seeds of insecurity in my mind, now so deeply rooted within me they may always haunt me. Some days I flash back to the things he embedded in my brain, feeling worthless and weak, but I've gotten better gradually. I'm the friend that others come to for advice, telling them what I think based on experiences that they know nothing about. My biggest piece of advice to them is if something doesn't feel right, it usually isn't. We like to make excuses for people we care about, but at some point, we have to quit making excuses and take up for ourselves. There's no excuse to be treated poorly – no one deserves to be lied to, cheated on, or pushed down. Despite what we may want to believe, the situation will likely never change. Although Collin tore my life completely apart, I have very few regrets. Collin made me appreciate everything so much more. Some days I wasn't sure if I was going to live to see the next. I hold onto myself now, and I have grown to love the person I have become. I used to hate looking in the mirror. I didn't recognize myself. I had lost sight of who I was while trying to fit a perfect mold. Now I look at myself and know that I can overcome whatever obstacle comes my way. If Collin gave me anything, he gave me the opportunity to see how strong I truly am. I will never lose myself again. I'm holding tight to everything I stand for, and I won't let go. I wish I knew how strong I could be a little sooner. What I didn't realize is that I didn't need a guy to get over Collin. Before, I was scared that nobody else would love me. Now, I'm focused on what I need and who I want to be, and through that, I have learned a lot about myself. I used to pretend to be this girl that I thought Collin wanted because I wanted his love so desperately. Now I don't try to be something that people want me to be. I don't care if people love me or not, I care about loving myself. Instead of playing a part of who others think I should be, I have taken comfort in who I truly am. I thought that being single meant being alone, but I'll always have a strong support system behind me whether I have a guy in my life or not. Being single was something that scared me a lot before. I've always known that life is nothing without love and happiness, but for a while I depended on Collin to give me those things. The truth is, it's not anyone else's job to make me feel whole – it's mine. I have learned how to feel whole on my own, and now nobody can ever take that away from me again.

www.ingramcontent.com/pod-product-compliance
Lightning Source LLC
Chambersburg PA
CBHW021934040426
42448CB00008B/1059